the Aspiring Mystic

Also by Carl McColman:

Spirituality: Where Body and Soul Encounter the Sacred

the Aspiring Mystic

Practical Steps
for Spiritual Seekers

Carl McColman

Adams Media Corporation
Holbrook, Massachusetts

Dedication

✳ Dedicated to everyone who attended Winter Celebration
at Massanetta Springs, Virginia, February 4–6, 1977. ✳

Published by
Adams Media Corporation
260 Center Street, Holbrook, MA 02343
www.adamsmedia.com

ISBN: 1-58062-416-2

Printed in Canada.

J I H G F E D C B A

Library of Congress Cataloging-in-Publication Data

McColman, Carl.
    The aspiring mystic : practical steps for spiritual seekers / Carl McColman.
        p.   cm.
    ISBN 1-58062-416-2
    1. Mysticism. I. Title.

BV5082.2 M23 2000
291.4'22—dc21   00-033193

This publication is designed to provide accurate and authoritative information with regard to the subject matter covered. It is sold with the understanding that the publisher is not engaged in rendering legal, accounting, or other professional advice. If legal advice or other expert assistance is required, the services of a competent professional person should be sought.
— From a Declaration of Principles jointly adopted by a Committee of the American Bar Association and a Committee of Publishers and Associations

Cover illustration by Michael Woloschinow/Marlena Agency

This book is available at quantity discounts for bulk purchases.
For information, call 1-800-872-5627.

Contents

Acknowledgments

Writing a book, like undergoing the spiritual journey, is a process that requires many friends, mentors, and supporters along the way.

I cannot even begin to list all the wonderful people who have aided my ongoing spiritual development—both in grand ways (such as serving as my spiritual director or soul friend) as well as very humble ways (recommending a book to me which would profoundly influence my faith). Only with the help of the many soul companions in my life could I ever have reached the point where I would dare to write a book about mysticism. You know who you are, and I thank you deeply.

This book never would have come to pass without the ongoing support of my literary agent, Linda Roghaar, and my editor, Paula Munier Lee. Several other folks, including Anne Weaver, Dawn Thompson, Denise Linn, and the late Gary Wilson, provided real encouragement along the way. Karen Price and Shirley Medley arranged my schedule at my "day job" to allow for as much time as possible to be devoted to the book.

Most of all, thanks to the two people who have been the most patient, loving, and nurturing to me throughout this process: my wife and stepdaughter. Fran and Rhiannon have endured many hours with me squirreled away in my home office, squinting into my monitor and tapping away at the keyboard. Living with a writer must be a trying task, and yet they continue to care for me with few complaints and much affection. Thank you both. The joy you bring to me, like the love of the Divine, simply cannot be put into words.

Author's Note

This is a book about mysticism. Therefore, it is a book about "God."

Sadly, that word has an inherently masculine meaning. While many people are comfortable with thinking of God as a father, others find the maleness of God to be a stumbling block. For this reason, I ask my readers to hold the word "God" lightly, especially in relation to gender.

Great mystics throughout history have spoken of God in both male and female ways. Following this tradition, we can explore both the maternal and paternal faces of the Divine, thereby experiencing the full range of ways in which the Spirit can lead us.

To say God is only masculine implies that God lacks the deeply feminine qualities of mothering, giving birth, and nurturing. Of course, it would be just as limiting to believe that the Sacred is only feminine. The truth about the Great Mystery is that, just as all life is teeming with gender and sexuality, so the Divine is a full manifestation of both masculine and feminine qualities.

I considered writing about "God and Goddess" or "Mother/Father God" or in some other way depicting God as more than just

a father figure. But in the end, I opted for simplicity. To my
readers who want a more inclusive name for the Divine, I ask your
forbearance. And for all readers, as a gentle reminder that God
means something far larger than our storybook images of the wise
old man who rules heaven, I also use descriptive nouns such as
"the Sacred" or "the Divine" or "the Great Mystery" to refer to that
which ultimately is beyond all names.

Chapter 1 # The Point of Departure

When I was 16 years old, I had an amazing experience. It involved an unasked-for and unexpected shift in my awareness and perception. This experience filled me with joy and serenity, which felt unlike anything I had ever experienced before. It was not merely a fleeting moment of ecstasy, but something that lingered for quite some time, perhaps half an hour or more. Exactly how long the experience lasted I cannot say, for among other things it altered my sense of time. But it endured long enough to make a lasting imprint in my soul; indeed, the afterglow of this experience remains with me to this day. My experience involved perceiving the presence of God. I saw God, I felt God, I knew God's pulsating presence within all things.

Several years would go by before I stumbled across the language to describe this event in my life. Eventually I learned to understand that experience this way: it was my first, and remains my most profound, mystical encounter with the Sacred. Whatever anyone may care to think about my experience, one thing is certain: it transformed my life. And now its impact has reached across the years to touch others, including you who now read these words. Perhaps you have been, or someday will be, transformed by your own mystical experience.

It occurred early in 1977, while I was attending a Lutheran youth conference called Winter Celebration. This annual event was held the first weekend of February at Massanetta Springs, a beautiful old Christian conference center nestled in the Shenandoah Valley of Virginia. I had been to numerous events at Massanetta over the years, and grew to love its stately, pre-Depression era charm. The center included a rambling old hotel with a large porch covered by rocking chairs, dozens of quaint cabins in the woods, and a large amphitheater where outdoor church services were held, with old classrooms filled with dusty Bibles where earnest teenagers would gather to discuss The Problems of Growing Up.

Going to Massanetta didn't just involve churchy stuff—there was a lake, a swimming pool, wonderful trails through the woods, a snack bar that served the best milkshakes in the world, and an overall sense of fun and adventure. Even the springs themselves—producing water which was bottled and sold as a cure-all back in the late nineteenth century—seemed special, like a North American version of an Irish Holy Well. Truly Massanetta Springs was a holy place, in the friendliest sense of the word. The name itself is partly derived from an Indian word meaning "a place of vision." It was as if God himself lived at Massanetta Springs, so going there meant getting closer to God.

Although most of my trips to Massanetta occurred in the summer when I could really enjoy the outdoors, this particular event marked my first visit to the center in wintertime. The valley was just as beautiful in February as in July, but it was an austere beauty, with a blanket of snow and a monastery-like silence. Rather than spending hours canoeing or swimming or hiking, Winter Celebration was a mostly indoor event, the hours spent getting to know the other kids who came from all over the state.

The highlight of the weekend was the Saturday night communion service. With all one hundred or so of the participants present, we'd have a long, comfortable, folk-style service, with plenty of singing as we stood arm in arm, swaying to the music. Although I had participated in such acoustic-guitar-driven worship services before, this one seemed different, from the start. As we sang, and eventually shared the bread and wine of Holy Communion, it seemed to me as if the entire room began to glow. Not a physical glowing, as if someone had turned on additional lights, but a radiance, a presence—words fail to describe. Slowly, but suddenly and obviously, things were different. Only words associated with light seem to capture the experience. Luminous, resplendent, glowing. It's as if everything—the walls of the room, the various people within it, the bread and the wine being passed from hand to hand—shimmered with a light that I could still perceive even when I closed my eyes. Call it energy, perhaps. It wasn't just as if there were a nonphysical light, it felt as if a new kind of love or joy had become manifest for the first time ever. I felt loved like I never had before. It seemed to me as if every person in the room became radiant with a visibly miraculous glow. Once I noticed it, I felt simply carried along by this serenity and joy that I had never felt before. It wasn't ecstasy, for I didn't feel like I left my body; nor was it a vision, for physically things appeared just as they always had. It had nothing to do with drugs; indeed when at a later date I experimented with LSD or cocaine or magic mushrooms, those substances always seemed pale and physically jarring in comparison to the loveliness I had known that night at Massanetta. Nor was it any kind of psychological breakdown—it had no ill effect on me physically or emotionally, other than to leave me with a sense of serenity and a feeling of connection to the God whom we were worshipping that evening.

This supernatural energy was so gut-level real to me, and so far beyond anything I might have imagined or tried to concoct, that I thought something objectively miraculous had happened in the room, some sort of profound moment in which God chose to reveal himself. By "objective," I mean I thought everyone must have experienced just what I did. Honestly. It never occurred to me that this might have been just a subjective experience! But I soon discovered to my surprise—and somewhat dismay—that others hadn't felt or seen anything at all unusual that evening. After the service ended, I said to two or three people, "Wasn't that *amazing?*" to which they responded with a totally noncommittal "Uh-huh." Soon I realized that, for some reason, I had been given a unique gift.

It happened at church camp, but this wasn't about church. I've been to plenty of church-sponsored events both before and since, and never did the windows of eternity open like they did that evening. No, it was something far deeper, far more profound, than mere religion.

Over the years that followed I became quite a seeker, looking for some way to make sense of that pivotal experience, to recapture it, or to cultivate new experiences like it. My search has led me from mainstream Protestant Christianity into the exciting spiritualism of Pentecostal and charismatic spirituality. It has led me to explore the great traditions of the east, such as Taoism and Zen Buddhism. It has led me to the earthy traditions of Native American shamanism, Celtic Paganism, and Wicca. I read philosophy, I tried psychedelic drugs, and I learned how to meditate. My search led me to monasteries and sweatlodges, Zen centers and stone circles, always on a quest for that undefinable something that seekers the world over call mystical experience.

My search never resulted in finding the Holy Grail. But I have learned a thing or two. I've discovered that mystical union with God is not something we can just conjure up, as if by magic. But I've also discovered there are basic principles of spirituality and mysticism that do not depend on the dogma of this or that religious tradition. True mysticism is a universal phenomenon that can flourish within any religion, any culture, any spirituality. Indeed, the mystic quest is the true heart of religion and the quest for the Sacred.

I have never had another experience as profound as the one that graced me that night in the winter of 1977. So if you have never had that kind of a "gee-whiz" experience, don't despair. I'm only one up on you, and that was many years ago. Since then, my spiritual experiences have been very small and humble, just like those of most spiritual seekers. But I've learned that, even though we cannot orchestrate Divine union, we can still do specific things to open our hearts and souls to the glorious winds of eternity. Maybe we won't see the face of God, but we can still feel the brush of his lips when he kisses us.

And that's what this book is about. How does a person go about the task of cultivating a spiritual consciousness? What steps do we need to take, regardless of our religious or philosophical background, to increase the likelihood of an encounter with Divine presence? How can we open ourselves up to at least the *possibility* of Divine union?

If these questions resonate with you, then you, like me, are what I call an "aspiring mystic." I'm not entirely comfortable calling myself a mystic, as if I've already arrived at a level of spiritual mastery equal to the Buddha or Christ. Obviously, I haven't, and I think I'm safe in assuming most of my readers haven't either. But the mystical life is certainly something I desire and hope to attain, and indeed have been trying to nurture with greater or lesser zeal ever since my initial shimmering experience.

There have been countless men and women who have devoted their entire lives to prayer, meditation, and the mystical quest, with never even a taste of ecstasy. So perhaps you and I, like them, will never graduate beyond aspiration. But unlike our results-oriented culture that sees value only in the big payoff, mysticism bestows as much reward on the pursuit as on the attainment. The old saying "success is not a destination, it's a journey" surely applies to the spiritual life. For me, the process of seeking spiritual enlightenment has been so rewarding and so lovely that even if I never get the goodies, I'm happy with the choices I've made in my life. Maybe that's easy for me to say, having had the good fortune of my one teenaged foray into profound mystic awareness. But I suspect that anyone who sincerely and earnestly embarks on the quest for Divine union will find that the journey is as worthy as the goal. For this reason, I am honored to be able to write this book, in which I invite you to join me in the greatest of all aspirations—to aspire for union with the heart of God.

From the Cave to the Sun

The great philosopher Plato once told a story about a group of people who were chained in a cave. The opening of the cave was behind them, and because of their chains they could never turn around and see the sunlight. All they could see was the play of light and shadow on the wall in front of them. For these enslaved souls, this shadow-play was what they experienced as "reality." Now it turned out that one person broke free from the chains and made it to the mouth of the cave. Outside for the first time, this person's eyes slowly adjusted to the sunlight and saw a brilliance of color and light that had not even been imagined before. It was almost as if the person had been transported into a higher state of ecstasy and perception.

The moral of the story is simple, and yet profound in its implication. We ordinary men and women who live our lives in the physical world of space, time, matter, and energy are like the chained souls trapped in the cave. We think what we see and experience is the totality of life—but perhaps all that we know is nothing more than shadows on a wall. Meanwhile, there seems to be a small number of spiritual explorers who manage to break out of the chains of normal perception, somehow reaching up to a world of higher, more beautiful perception of things infinite and eternal. These visionary explorers are the people called "mystics." They are the true spiritual pioneers of the human race.

Who wouldn't like to truly experience union with the mind and heart of God? To be ushered into the presence of the Creator, to the source of infinite power and love before which people have bowed and worshiped for millennia? What could be more amazing than to become so fully connected with the Divine that our consciousness literally merged with God?

If this sounds a little too churchy, take heart. Not everyone feels comfortable with such high-sounding religious language. So here's another way to frame these questions: Have you ever wished you could truly—and I mean *truly*—comprehend the highest possibilities of human thought and perception? Like the person who escaped Plato's cave, wouldn't you love to ascend to a higher plane of experience, a place where you could truly apprehend the uncreated source of love and life and light? Imagine how it must feel to have your fields of vision and awareness suddenly transformed into the shimmering radiance of union with the beating heart of the universe—to encounter a cosmic force more powerful than gravity and more funda- mental than life or death—to immediately feel the pulsation of pure joy and passion flood your bones and veins in a way that makes the pleasure of such things as drugs or even sex seem pale and insignificant?

Do you long to find the meaning of life? Do you believe that such a thing as spiritual truth exists, somewhere, somehow? Do you suspect that a greater purpose just might exist for humanity as a whole, and for each of us as individuals, a purpose beyond the limits of human understanding . . . and do you yearn to understand this greater purpose for yourself?

Do you meditate or pray regularly—or do you wish you could? Are you intrigued by silence, or by solitude, or by such quiet places as gardens or cathedrals or even forests in the morning? Are you so comfortable with silence, that even the silence of darkness, of doubt, and of unknowing strike you as being full of wisdom and meaning?

If you answer "yes"—or perhaps even "maybe"—to any of these questions, you are an aspiring mystic.

What Is a Mystic?

A mystic is a person who explores the spiritual mysteries of life. A mystic seeks to break free from the limitations of thought, feeling, and perception that have been imposed on us by the ordinary, everyday, work-to-survive world we live in, breaking free in order to encounter and experience a higher, deeper, eternal truth.

The word "mystic" stems from the Greek word *mystes*. A *mystes* is someone who has been initiated into spiritual mysteries. In the ancient world, spiritual seekers would often undergo an initiation into secret or hidden truths associated with a God or Goddess. These hidden truths empowered the initiate to live a happier, more abundant, or more meaningful life. The ancient practices associated with such spiritual secrets were known as mystery religions, and only the initiate—the mystic—could possess the hidden truths.

Nowadays we live in a much more open spiritual climate. Although some secretive religious or fraternal groups still exist, for the most part we are used to spiritual ideas being available to anyone who wants them. From the Methodists to the Taoists, almost all religious or spiritual organizations offer their teachings openly, in a public manner. Mysticism is no longer reserved for the elite few—it's available to anyone and everyone. No secrets, no hidden teachings.

But just because we don't have any spiritual *secrets* any more does not mean there are no longer any spiritual *mysteries*. To be sure, mystery remains a central part of spirituality—regardless of the tradition. Mystery lies at the heart of the spiritual questions we ask: What is the ultimate meaning of life? It's a mystery. What is the true nature of love? It's a mystery. Why is there suffering, fear, rage, and pain in our world? Another mystery. What happens after we die? Again, it's a mystery. Many individuals, groups, and traditions have their theories about what lies beyond these mysteries—indeed, you could say that all of the sacred teachings, writings, and rituals of every religious tradition in the world are attempts to solve the mysteries of existence—but in the end, no one person or tradition can truly be said to have the final say. The mysteries are simply bigger than our best attempts to vanquish them.

A mystic is a person willing to grapple with the deep mysteries of life, even though this means entering the realm of the unknown and unknowable. A mystic willingly spends his or her entire life yearning to comprehend the nature of God, seeking to foster a sense of connectedness with the Sacred, trying to understand and apply the laws of the Divine to everyday life. A mystic knows that these mysteries stand at the threshold of darkness and unknowing, of doubt and fear. Mystical spirituality is not a cozy little program someone can complete in a weekend workshop! Mysticism takes a lifetime, for the mysteries of life are huge and can never be fully understood, let alone "solved." But even though these mysteries are so deep and so vast, that doesn't stop the mystical seeker from exploring them. Mystical seekers trust that entering into the deepest mysteries will yield true spiritual awareness—an experience that will not only transform their own lives, but even benefit the lives of others.

Questions, Questions, Questions

What does it really mean to enter life's deepest mysteries? What kinds of spiritual awareness or vision might a mystic possess? How can I reach the level of consciousness and experience that can truly be called mystical? How do I even know if God exists, and if so, what can I truly expect from God? What difference will it make to be a mystic?

If questions like these are beginning to turn over in your mind, you are now standing at the brink of the mystical realm.

You are standing at the place Evelyn Underhill, one of the great mystics of the twentieth century, called the "Point of Departure." As you begin to wrestle with these questions, seeking answers and finding that each answer causes new questions to be formed, you will embark on a lifelong journey, a quest for spiritual wisdom and power and freedom—and, most of all, love. You are standing at the edge of a place where your knowledge and awareness will be stretched to their limits, where you are able to catch glimpses of the vast universe of unknowing that stretches beyond. You are standing at the edge of a place where the presence of the Sacred— the One, the Great Mystery—may be discerned. You are standing at a *liminal* place—an in-between place—in between dazzling light and impenetrable darkness, in between infinite beauty and the inscrutable human capacity for horror, in between the places where angels and demons, gods and goddesses, fairies and devas, make their home.

If you are like me, you find this place at the edge of mystery to be tremendously exciting. Although it is a journey "inward"—into the realms of imagination and consciousness, into the place where our mind and body connect to our soul and spirit—it is as exciting as any journey into the wilderness or the desert or the rugged mountains. It is exciting because it is a journey into the unknown.

Many people have gone before us on this journey into mystery. They are the mystics, great and humble, who have lived throughout history. The greatest ones are familiar to almost everyone: Jesus, the Buddha, Mohammed, Francis of Assisi. Their wisdom and teachings were so deeply imbued with Divine understanding that they are now recognized and respected in many cultures and traditions, the world over.

Other mystics are less well known, but no less great; they often have reputations at least within their own tradition. For example, in the Christian religion there is a long history of great visionaries and spiritual explorers who dedicated their life to the quest for union with God. Some of these people included Hildegard of Bingen (a German nun who lived in the twelfth century), Julian of Norwich (an English woman from the fourteenth century), and Teresa of Avila (a Spanish nun from the sixteenth century). These people, and many others like them, not only devoted their life to prayer, meditation, and service to humanity, but also wrote books about their spiritual experiences that are now classic works of mystical insight. These are the spiritual heroes and heroines who have experienced visions of God or supernatural transformations of consciousness or awareness, who have lived lives of heroic virtue, fueled by their extraordinary connectedness to Spirit.

What Is an "Aspiring Mystic"?

I'm an *aspiring* mystic because I know I have not come anywhere near the level of wisdom or power or love that was manifested in the lives of the great mystics like Francis of Assisi or Julian of Norwich. I don't want to mislead anyone into thinking this book is a shortcut to Divine ecstasy and bliss. It isn't. Although some spiritual teachers may promise a path to instant enlightenment, my intuition tells me it is better to trust the mystics like Teresa of Avila, who insist that spiritual attainment requires commitment, perseverance, and courage—and may take a lifetime.

My experience, like the experience of all the aspiring mystics I know, is similar to that of a person who aspires to be an Olympic athlete. Spirituality, like sports, requires discipline and training in order to make progress. With training and discipline, an ordinary person is capable of cultivating a degree of mystical consciousness—that's been true for me, and I believe the advice in this book will help you to manifest it in your life as well. But keep in mind how most athletes, even with dedicated discipline and training, never reach the level of achievement an Olympian attains. So it is with mysticism—only a few people in any age are called to the heights of mystery and spiritual vision attained by Teresa or Julian.

But just because I'll never be an Olympic athlete is no reason for me to stop working out. I know that my body benefits from exercise, no matter what I do—or don't—achieve. Sports, ultimately, are about enjoyment, not achievement (we forget this in our hypercompetitive society, but it's true). Spirituality works the same way. Now, don't say that you'll *never* be a great mystic, for unlike athletes who almost always achieve their pinnacle in the first half of life, mystical awareness can flood a soul at any point, from infancy to old age. But it really doesn't matter if you or I ever reach the same level as Francis. We can find beauty and spiritual purpose in the striving itself—and, from the perspective of the Sacred, whatever level we do ultimately achieve is good enough.

So that's why I call myself an aspiring mystic. I aspire to bathe my heart and mind, my body and soul, in the loving presence of the Great Mystery. I may or may not scale the highest summits in this life. But I'll try. And ultimately, since my goal is to love and be loved by the Sacred, I know the real point lies not in the results I achieve, but in the choices I make in the process.

Come with me. Whether you are new to this business of spirituality, or are an old-timer like me, I hope my ideas will spark some enthusiasm and vision within yourself. In this book, I share some of the basic lessons I've learned in over 20 years of spiritual seeking and intentional practice. It's not meant to imply that I am an "expert." Actually, I believe the further one travels down the path of the mystic, the more conscious he or she will become of being just a beginner, always a beginner. So I call myself a beginner, but at least with a few years' experience. I hope some of the things I've learned over the years can be helpful to you on your own quest for spiritual meaning and happiness.

In writing this book, I've tried to balance two ways of approaching the mystical life. First is the simple narrative of a book about spirituality. You might think writing about the inner life would be the most natural thing to do, but you would not believe how challenging it is! It's not like trying to describe how an engine works or instructions on how to construct an outhouse. Mysticism is organic, fluid, and somewhat chaotic, defying the left-brained logic of beginning-middle-end. So the pages to come have a bit of a rambly, meandering feel to them, for that seems to me the best way to capture the true nature of the spiritual life—a relationship with the Infinite tends to be a rambly, unpredictable affair.

But I want this to be a practical book. How can the meanderings of the mystic way translate into practical steps for spiritual seekers? To do this, I've relied on that marvelous invention of contemporary page layout—the shaded box. So as you meander with me through my ideas and anecdotes, you'll come across shaded boxes, each of which has a specific recommendation of something to do, to take you that much further down your path.

So, let's go explore!

Getting Started

Cookbook recipes begin with a list of ingredients: the materials needed to follow the recipe and successfully prepare a meal. If mysticism could be compared to cooking, here are the "ingredients" you'll need:

* *A journal*
* *A place and time for regular, uninterrupted silence*
* *A candle, an icon, or some other symbol for the Sacred (optional)*
* *Sacred writings from one or more of the world's great wisdom traditions (optional)*

It really is this simple. Keeping a journal helps to develop awareness and memory. Becoming aware of the spiritual dimension of life, and learning to remember the patterns of spiritual growth and development we undergo, are essential for anyone wishing to develop mystical consciousness. The place and time for silence is your own "mini-monastery," a place of retreat and refuge from the noisiness of modern life. Silence is to a mystic what soil is to a tulip: in other words, essential for growth. Sacred writings and symbols, while technically not necessary, still help a person to cultivate his or her sense of connection to the spiritual world.

There are other important elements to mystical spirituality, such as a supportive community. But these basic tools will get you started.

Practical Step: Set aside a place in your home where you can cultivate your mystical spirituality. Keep your journal and meditation supplies handy. Make agreements with your family or housemates to have uninterrupted silent time in your mystic place, ideally on a daily basis.

Chapter 2 # Extraordinary Moments

In the fourteenth century in eastern England lived a woman who has become the most famous mystic of her land. We don't even know her name, for when her book was published, she simply identified herself by the name of the church where she lived. It was customary for holy men and women at that time to live in enclosed cells attached to churches, where they could participate in the worship of the church, and dispense wisdom and spiritual advice to the people of the town. This woman lived in a cell attached to the Church of St. Julian in the town of Norwich, and so she is now known as Julian of Norwich.

Julian was born in 1342, and lived possibly as late as 1412 or so. She survived several outbreaks of the plague, and other calamities such as peasant uprisings and war between England and France. But she almost didn't survive at all past her thirtieth year. She tells in her book, *Revelations of Divine Love*, how she came down with a serious illness in May 1373; so serious, in fact, that a priest was called to administer last rites. The priest came to the woman on her sickbed, and held a crucifix before her, instructing her to gaze on the image of Jesus so that he might comfort her as she died. But what happened next was beyond anything she could have imagined. As she gazed on the crucifix, suddenly the blood pouring from the crown of thorns on Jesus was real blood. When she saw this, she felt filled with a supernatural joy she understood as coming from the Divine in heaven. From there, she experienced vision after vision of God, Jesus, the Virgin Mary, and even of the Spirit of Evil. The visions were lifelike, vivid, and filled with meaning, as she conversed with God and received lesson after spiritual lesson. The overall theme of her visions (or showings, as she called them) was the magnificence and totality of Divine Love. In the morning, against all expectations, her fever broke and she began to recuperate from her illness.

Julian wrote a brief recounting of her visions not long after experiencing them. But as the years went by and she adopted the life of the holy woman living in the cell at St. Julian's Church, she prayed and reflected on the meaning of her experience. Twenty years went by, and she finally recounted the spiritual meaning and lessons of her showings in the final version of her book—the first book by a woman written in the English language.

As best we know, Julian only had the one mystical experience. Granted, as mystical experiences go it was truly extraordinary, but Julian never hints at any other event of Divine awareness. Instead, she devotes the rest of her life to mulling over what she has been shown and how she can pass along her lessons to others.

I don't suppose many people have experiences as spectacular as Julian's. But I do believe mystical experiences are far more common than most people will readily acknowledge. Indeed, I suspect just about everyone has had multiple experiences and events of transcendent awareness that deserve to be called mystical.

Moments of Wonder

Think of a time, maybe when you were young or maybe more recently—a time when you stood in some sort of natural setting such as a park or a forest, or perhaps even a mountaintop bluff looking out over a lush valley—and you really, deeply, became connected and attuned with nature. It felt almost as if you and the object of your attention were at one. Maybe you noticed the brilliant blue sky, covering the earth like a lovely hung tapestry; maybe you saw brilliant, sparkling cumulus clouds, with sunlight pouring over them in golden waves of illumination; maybe you noticed a majestic oak tree as if it were the first time you ever saw such a creature, with thousands of branches and leaves reaching out in countless ways, all struggling to bask in the radiant sunlight. Maybe you became filled with wonder at something very small, like a turtle slowly making its way over the ground in search of a meal and a safe place to rest, or a squirrel, playfully darting from tree to ground and back to tree, busily gathering nuts both to eat and to hide away for the coming winter.

Whatever it was that you saw, in gazing at this natural wonder you became one with it. You connected with it on such a deep level that all time and space seemed to drop away, even if only for a moment. In fact, even the boundaries within your mind that separate "you" from "nature" seemed to disappear, even if only temporarily.

Does this remind you of an experience you've had? I hope so. Indeed, I'm confident that everyone who reads these words has had such an experience, possibly many times. If someone cannot recall such a moment of wonder, then my guess is that he or she either uses different words than I do to describe connecting with nature, or else may have chosen to forget such experiences, either because life is too busy, or too burdened with pain and suffering, or maybe because he or she never thought such moments of natural ecstasy were very important and so just ignored them.

Take as much time as possible to recall the moments of wonder in your life. It doesn't matter if it happened yesterday, or when you were three years old. Simply allow yourself to recall a time when you were so caught up in the amazingness of things that you forgot yourself. Now, take a moment to reconnect your mind and body with how it felt. In your imagination and awareness, open up to what you saw, what you felt, what you may have thought (or not thought). Allow yourself as best you can to relive the encounter with wonder.

One of my earliest experiences of oneness with nature occurred when I was 10 years old. My brother, sister-in-law, and I were walking along the edge of Lake Gaston in southern Virginia. It was the morning of July 5, and the beach was littered with bottle rockets from the festivities the night before. As a budding environmentalist I felt sad about the litter, but even that sadness could not detract from the overall sense of connection I felt with the lake and the trees surrounding it. I felt like I was in love with the lake; she was a beautiful, nurturing companion to us, playfully sparkling as the sunlight danced on her rippling surface. The sand

and dirt beneath our feet crunched with a familiar feel and sound as we walked along, and the trees stood like silent friends, their "arms" waving gently to us in the breeze as we walked by. I had been to this lake many times before, but on this day, nature seemed to transform herself into a luminous place of love, serenity, and safety. I felt like I was truly at home, truly loved, and truly at peace.

Several years later, something similar happened while I was driving to work one morning. I was listening to classical music on the radio, and every time I stopped at a red light I gazed at the sky. I was driving westward, so the early morning sun made the clouds ahead of me shimmer with yellows and pinks and bluish-white tints. The beautiful music combined with the beauty of nature made me wish my entire body could expand to take it all in, to be filled with the loveliness that I saw and heard. I felt so very small, in a world of such large beauty—but it wasn't a bad feeling, it was again a feeling like falling in love.

I'm not talking about full-blown mystical visions of the face of God. Neither my experience at the lake nor driving to work was anything like my experience at Winter Celebration. These moments of nature-ecstasy simply were times when peace, wonder, love, and joy seemed very present. My socks weren't knocked off, but for a moment I forgot about all my cares and simply basked in how good it felt to be alive. I felt happy and safe.

Such moments of wonder and ecstasy seem to course through our very bones, connecting our bodies and souls to the universe surrounding us. In this connection, this "at-oneness" with nature, we encounter the *numinous*. Numinous is a Greek word meaning "of the Divine." A numinous experience transforms a person with wonder and unity to the point where she feels as if she has no limits, no boundaries separating the self from the universe from the Sacred. Numinous experiences range from the humble, simple, moments of joy or serenity, to the powerful, knock-your-socks-off-and-blow-your-fuses events of energy flowing and surging through your veins as your consciousness seems forever transformed from the mundane to the transcendent. Most of my encounters with the numinous have occurred while communing with nature, but they could happen in the middle of a grimy city or a pleasant suburb, they could happen while caring for a baby

Hearing the Numinous

The ears can be just as powerful as the eyes to cultivating mystical consciousness. Listening to music can have profound physiological and spiritual effects on a person, including the possibility of transporting the listener into states of ecstasy.

Shamans have always known that a steady drumbeat can induce a trance state. Modern dance and "rave" music, often produced with over one hundred beats a minute, when played at loud volumes can induce dreamlike states of consciousness. Even the pipe organ, under the gifted hands of a composer like J. S. Bach, can be an instrument for evoking the experience of ecstasy.

The power of music extends beyond the physiological experience of altered consciousness. The delicate beauty of a violin sonata or a

flute concerto can bring tears of joy to a receptive listener. Euphoria of a different kind may be found in the sexy, gritty, urban vibe of jazz or soul.

Only you can decide which kind of music best supports your quest for eternity. However, here are some musical works that I personally have found to be especially conducive to mystical yearning:

* *Ralph Vaughan Williams*, Fantasia on a Theme by Thomas Tallis
* *Ludwig van Beethoven*, Ninth Symphony
* *Johann Sebastian Bach*, Toccata and Fugue in D Minor
* *John Coltrane*, A Love Supreme
* *Van Morrison*, Astral Weeks

Practical Step: *Go through your collection of tapes or CDs (or that of a friend, if you don't collect music). What music do you find to be spiritually uplifting? Make a habit of listening to that kind of music as much as possible. Think of music not only as entertainment, but as a sonic gift to your soul. Listen to music that honors your soul—avoid music filled with negative lyrics.*

or an elderly relative, or even while having a dream in which you can fly!

It can happen in church. It can happen while watching a woman give birth. It can happen while working in the garden. It can happen while stuck in traffic. Encounters with the wonder that usher us into the numinous are not predictable or controllable. They simply happen. The little ones feel good, and the big ones transform us.

Although I've been describing joyful or "positive" encounters with the numinous, such moments where eternity seems to encounter us may also happen during the shadow times of life. Grief, suffering, fear, or rage may all be doorways into the infinite as surely as love, joy, and peace may be. The Angel of Wonder can seek us out in any area of our life—happy or sad, beautiful or horrifying, serene or troubled. Eternity, after all, is bigger than our emotions, bigger than our division of things into "good" and "bad"!

Acknowledge the existence of the numinous. Acknowledge how it is possible to suddenly notice something—anything—outside of yourself that triggers within you a sense of eternity, of connectedness, of unity with something larger than yourself. As you read through this book over the days to come, you may find it helpful to keep a journal or a diary; use it to record your memories of your numinous experiences. Try not to judge how big or spectacular they are; even a small moment of fleeting ecstasy counts. And if at first you don't remember any, don't fret. As you begin to explore your inner life more fully, you will be surprised at the memories of wonder or awe that will surface. Chances are, you'll also find yourself blessed with new experiences of the numinous. Try not to analyze or "figure out" such experiences. Just remember the peak experiences of your past, and when you have such experiences in the future, simply notice them. Notice them, and be thankful for them.

Control the Urge to Control

We mortals like to be in control. So naturally, when it comes to mysticism, the first thing we want to do is to control our experiences of ecstasy, unity, and wonder. Once we learn how to recognize the moments of numinous encounter, we tend to assume that such experiences can occur at our beck and call. Or, perhaps, we assume they only occur at certain locations, under certain circumstances. Once we've had an experience or two of Divine joy or ecstasy (or any kind of heartfelt spiritual perception), it's easy to assume we have therefore figured out the nature of mysticism. In order to experience the magic again, all we have to do is re-create the circumstances in which we experienced Divine ecstasy the first time. And nothing else will do. So, if you've had a sense of the presence of God while partaking in Holy Communion at a Catholic church, you may think that's where God lives, and it's the only way to encounter him. But you may just as easily have had an extraordinary feeling of Sacred peace while out walking in the forest, which may lead you to conclude that it's easier to find God in nature than in a church. Whatever circumstances may surround your initial forays into the mystical world, there's always this incredible temptation to assume you've got God figured out and you can have a mystical experience, just by re-enacting the circumstances that catapulted you into the mystery the first time.

But it doesn't work that way.

Unfortunately, we cannot just manufacture a mystical experience, like a magician pulling a rabbit out of a hat. We can do things to make experiences of wonder and ecstasy *more likely*— such as a daily practice of prayer and meditation, or making time for a retreat from our normal routine, or making real efforts to help others (all topics to be covered in the pages to come). In fact, the "job" of an aspiring mystic is precisely that: to create an open, flexible space in his or her mind, body, and soul, a space where such encounters with the Sacred may be possible.

But none of this comes with a guarantee. Remember, ecstasy and mysticism involves two parties: you and the object of your attention. Whether you are uniting with nature or with the limitless majesty of God, you are not the only party in the experience of ecstasy. Just because you are willing to receive an experience of wonder doesn't mean that life will automatically grant it to you. God may have other plans for you at that moment, or may decide that you will grow faster without the benefit of a "gee-whiz" peak experience. On the other hand, when you least expect it, a magnificent, life-transforming experience of mystical union may explode within your awareness.

Encountering the numinous is a lot like being in love. You may love another person, and you can hope she loves you, and you can ask her to love you. But you cannot make her love you. Mysticism works the same way. You can love the mystery, and you can hope for and ask for an experience of the Sacred within that mystery. But you cannot make it happen.

Another point to remember, as I mentioned previously, is that both the positive and negative aspects of life can be a setting for an encounter with the eternal. But spiritual seekers often think about the Sacred so much in terms of "light" and "love" and "joy" that we begin to think God only comes to us in happy ways, in peaceful settings, or in the beauty of nature.

It's an unfortunate mistake to assume that light and nature and love and wonder are mystical qualities, while fear and doubt and urban grime are therefore "un-mystical." Nothing could be further from the truth. Mystical or numinous experiences can (and do) break through in the dark as well as the light, in times of great fear or doubt or pain just as in times of joy or happiness, in the unglamorous world of a city slum just as easily as on the mountaintop. Why have the great saints and mystics of the world—people like Francis of Assisi or Mother Teresa—been so quick to work with the sick and the poor and the suffering? For two reasons: They do it out of gratitude for the love they have received from the Sacred, and because *they know the Sacred presence can be found in the most broken places in our society*—often much more easily there than at the fancy weekend workshop featuring this month's celebrity guru.

Everyone tries to control the Sacred—it's part of human nature. If you are serious about walking the mystical path, sooner or later you will catch yourself trying to be in control. When you catch yourself trying to make mystical experiences happen according to your whims and desires, simply take a deep breath and let it go. And don't assume that the Sacred only comes in certain ways or in certain places. Look into the sky, or gaze into the ocean, and notice how vast such natural things are. Remember the Sacred is larger than the entire universe. When it comes to the mystical way, you are very small and humble; you are the small end of the equation. It is good to bear this in mind.

Create the Space for Miracles

Perhaps you're thinking something along these lines: "All right, so each of us has our momentary glimpses of eternity, our transitory sense of unity and ecstasy that we feel in response to a beautiful scene of nature or a miracle like watching a baby's birth. But mysticism is more than just a sensation of wonder, right? So how do I experience the depth of a true mystical experience, like Julian of Norwich did?"

In response, here are two thoughts. First, we need to remember that the only difference between a big mystical experience and a little mystical experience is size. In other words, we who aspire to the mystical life can celebrate the little miracles, rather than waste time comparing ourselves to the spiritual giants like the Buddha who had big miracles. The comparison game is always a losing proposition, for we'll always find someone who's a bigger, more evolved mystic than we are (just like there's always someone who makes more money, has more sex, is better looking, etc., etc.). Mysticism is about quality, not quantity. Notice and enjoy the moments of ecstasy in your life, and if they are little moments, so what? A small window onto eternity has the same view as one of large plate glass.

Second, if we want to cultivate a truly mystical spirituality, then we need to create the space for it in our lives. We need to open ourselves up to the possibility not only of ecstasy and wonder, but truly of miracles happening within us. So the next step after noticing our capacity for ecstasy is to begin taking steps to open up our lives to create the space for more wonder to flow in.

Even Julian of Norwich did this. At the beginning of her book, she admits that she "desired a vision" before she ever got sick and received the showings. Because she lived in medieval Christian Europe, she understood a vision to involve the love of God, the suffering of Jesus, and the compassion of the Virgin Mary. Mystics from other traditions would use other words and images to express their desire for the Sacred. Julian was handsomely rewarded for her desire—she received not one, but 16, revelations of Divine Love.

If a mystic has attained union with the Infinite, then we aspiring mystics may start our journey into ecstatic spirituality simply by declaring, "I desire union with the Divine for myself." Even making a simple intention like this can set into motion the energetics of mystical transformation.

Does this strike you as a little kooky? (Be honest!) I admit, I've had a hard time giving myself permission to make such a grandiose statement. Well, maybe in the jaded and cynical eyes of our postmodern world it *is* a little kooky to believe in the possibility of mystical experience. If that's the case, then so be it. Once upon a time it was kooky to believe that the earth was round, or that humankind could fly, or that we could put a man on the moon. Again and again, human knowledge and ability has overcome the cynics and the naysayers. If we can plumb the mysteries of the atom, who says we cannot also scale the heights to gaze into the eyes of the gods?

Those of us who want to make that climb and who seek that vision can take great comfort in the words of those who have gone before us, whether ancient mystics like Julian of Norwich or Francis of Assisi, world teachers like Jesus or Buddha, or even spiritual masters of recent years like the Catholic monk Thomas Merton or the Indian guru Sathya Sai Baba. Each of these visionaries have either committed their own words to paper, or have had followers who have preserved their wisdom for others to read and learn.

What are the patterns that emerge when we look at the teachings of mystics from different times and places? Here are some of the key themes of mystical literature from the world over.

* A mystic desires supernatural union with the Sacred;
* A mystic willingly undergoes spiritual discipline;
* A mystic encounters mystery, and accepts the unknowing;
* A mystic experiences some sort of ecstatic union with the Divine, and as a result, his or her life is forever transformed.

So mysticism involves four essential steps: desire, willingness, encounter, and transformation. Now, the circumstances and specific language or imagery a mystic uses to describe his or her experience will always be shaped by whatever tradition or religion that mystic is connected to. In other words, a Christian, Jewish, or Muslim mystic might seek union with God, while a Hindu or Buddhist mystic may seek pure enlightenment without thinking in terms of union with a deity. A Neopagan or Wiccan mystic might seek union with the Goddess, or maybe just with nature or the universe. And of course, not only is the *object* of their mystical desires different, but the *experiences* that each mystic will encounter will also seem different, again because they are shaped and colored by the culture in which the mystic lives and moves.

What separates aspiring mystics from everybody else in the world is the degree of commitment we have to the first of the essential steps: that desire for supernatural union with the Sacred. This arises out of the moments of spontaneous ecstasy and wonder that we have been considering. In recognizing the mysterious moments, great or small, in our lives when we were caught up out of ourselves into something larger, more eternal, and more loving, it is possible to believe such ecstasy exists without limitations or hindrances. If it feels wonderful to gaze at a sunset, how must it feel to gaze at the source of pure love? If seeing a person suffer elicits in me a feeling of compassion, how much more profound is the compassion of the Sacred—and how much more profound would my compassion be, if I were united with the eternal Source? If life seems filled with shimmering beauty because of the numinous mystery you encounter in a blossoming flower, how much more radiance may be seen in the mystery of pure Divine being, pure Divine power and creativity? These are questions a mystic asks, and these questions will accompany you as you travel along this visionary path.

Mystical experiences, from the tiniest fleeting glimpse of ecstasy all the way up to the boundless visions such as those granted to Julian of Norwich, are *always* miraculous. The only difference between a little miracle and a big miracle is size. The ecstasy in your life, whether fleeting and tiny or long-lasting and earth-shattering, always has a miraculous quality about it. This is the next step on the mystical journey. After noticing the ordinary moments of wonder in your life, recognize that these moments have an essentially miraculous quality about them.

I remember the first time I saw a waterfall. I was a small boy, and my parents and I were travelling across New York state. We spent the night at Niagara Falls, and since we arrived there after dark I didn't see the waterfalls until the morning. But when I did . . . wow! It was truly a moment of ecstasy. But it was also a moment of amazement, as I gazed onto the thunderous power of so much water rushing over the falls, never stopping, never resting. That so much water even existed seemed amazing to my little mind. That such power was present in nature also fired my imagination. And I also noticed the sheer beauty of the rainbows dancing in the mist and spray. To me, the waterfalls were miraculous. They lifted me out of my normal state of mind to a fleeting glimpse of a higher, more wondrous consciousness. And I've come to see the traces of miracles in every place where I see wonder—from the sparkling eyes of a loved one to the celestial tapestry of a sunset.

Thanks to Cecil B. DeMille and George Lucas, we sometimes make the mistake of thinking something is a miracle only if it involves God's special effects department. And maybe that goes back to ancient myth and sacred scriptures, where miracles of the supernatural variety abound. But an event doesn't have to suspend the laws of nature in order to be miraculous. Truly whenever we experience wonder, we are susceptible to noticing the presence of the Infinite; and that is what makes a miracle. Indeed, "miracle" comes from the Latin *mirari*, which means "to wonder at"! So a miracle is a wonderful event, no matter how grand or simple. Sure, a supernatural event like walking on water or raising the dead would be a miracle. But suddenly seeing eternity in the delicate petals of a rose blossom is just as miraculous. Whether the miracles you encounter are great or small (and the testimony of both great and ordinary mystics reminds us that miracles come in all shapes and sizes), remember that behind and beneath all of your experiences of wonder, you may find the movement of the Sacred. Think of miracles as chinks in the armor of our normal mundane awareness. Through those chinks, if we care or dare to look, we will see the splendor of Divine radiance.

The Supernatural Pitfall

Okay, so if the miracle of a baby's laugh is so great, wouldn't it be even better—more miraculous, and therefore more mystical—to experience a true supernatural event, such as levitating, or having visions of God, or manifesting flowers out of thin air?

Here's the biggest temptation we will face as we begin our journey into the mystical life: the journey to equate mysticism with supernatural abilities or experiences. Yes, many mystics have had amazing and extraordinary experiences that defy all the laws of physics. Yes, I believe such signs and wonders really do happen, and are possible. But does it really make sense to devote our energy to chasing after such spiritual pyrotechnics?

Many mystics would say not. In sixteenth-century Spain, a great mystic named John of the Cross wrote several books on the spiritual life. In one of these, called *The Ascent of Mount Carmel*, he had these words to say on the matter of supernatural miracles: "Heavenly visions and revelations are not worth as much as the smallest act of humility . . . therefore do not try to find happiness in these supernatural experiences, but seek to forget them for the sake of being free."

Meanwhile, in the Zen tradition, the concept of *makyo* refers to psychic or paranormal experiences that a student may experience while meditating. Zen masters warn their disciples to ignore such experiences, for they are distractions to the pursuit of true meditation.

Great mystics from different traditions have often cautioned their students to avoid becoming caught up in the quest for supernatural miracles or paranormal experiences. Even though many mystics have themselves been surrounded by extraordinary phenomena, they emphasize that such amazing events are merely the window dressing of the more central experience—union with the Sacred. And the great mystics insist that such union is possible, even without the supernatural events. In other words, don't assume that you must be surrounded by visions, voices, and jaw-dropping events in order to be a mystic. In fact, for many people, extraordinary experiences might be a distraction, rather than an aid, to the quest for true spiritual maturity.

The idea that you must experience supernatural miracles in order to be united with the Divine is like saying you must have a million dollars in order to be wealthy. Sure, having a million dollars would be very nice, and most people would assume that a millionaire is wealthy. But think for a moment about who you would *rather* be: a millionaire whose life is filled with paranoia and suspicion of others, always trying to protect his fortune from theft or calamity—or a modest farmer who makes just enough to get by, but whose life is filled with joy and gratitude for the goodness of the land, and whose home is always filled with laughter and good times thanks to family and friends?

You don't have to be a rocket scientist to figure out which one is truly wealthy. True wealth resides in the heart, not in the bank. The same goes for the mystical life. In fact, one way to think of mysticism is as "spiritual abundance." You could be witness to amazing supernatural events, from physically seeing angels to witnessing someone raised from the dead—but if you have not allowed Sacred love to flow in your heart, what good is it? On the other hand, you may go through your life with never a hint of anything supernatural, but with your body and soul singing with the music of the spheres. That is truly the way of the mystic.

The old saying "attitude is everything" applies here. The choices you make in your heart will do more to further you on the mystical path than anything you ever see, hear, or experience. Of course, by choosing to open yourself to the love and the presence of the Sacred, you are opening yourself up to the miraculous—and sooner or later, it's possible that a big miracle may well transform your entire world. Or, just as likely, the "big one" may never come. Don't worry about that. Focus on choosing love and joy, and praying for the Sacred to transform your life in healing and compassionate ways.

Nurture Your Dreams

If the first step on the mystical path is desiring union with God, that desire often manifests itself as dreams we harbor—often idealistic, visionary dreams we keep guarded and secret, where they remain safe from the ridicule of skeptics and cynics.

Have you ever dreamt of a world where people live in harmony with one another and with creation, where conflict is managed responsibly and creatively, where every person manifests his or her fullest creative potential? Have you dreamt that our world could be filled with unending abundance and prosperity, so that no one would go hungry or would want for anything, thereby making crime and violence obsolete?

Have you ever dreamt of opening yourself up so fully to the moments of Divine wonder that characterize the mystical life, that such moments no longer seem fleeting and transitory, but rather fill your entire being with a sense of ecstasy—even just a humble, quiet, and serene ecstasy—most or even all of the time? Have you dreamt of loving God with such power, devotion, and consciousness that you remain aware of the Sacred presence in your life on an ongoing basis?

These are the dreams of the mystic. By embarking on the mystic quest, we declare to the universe that we are dreamers and we believe in our dreams—we believe in universal peace and harmony and love and spiritual power. To believe in our dreams means to declare that "what could be" is more important to us, a more central guiding force, than "what is." We choose to live our lives in such a way as to constantly strive for cultivating a better world, not only for ourselves, but also for what Native Americans call "all our relations"—family, friends, loved ones, as well as the larger community of humankind and even the plant, animal, and mineral kingdoms.

Dare to dream—and keep your dreams alive. Dare to go after them! This is not necessarily the easiest advice to follow, for the world we live in does not always support the dream of a mystic. We are taught at a young age to be practical and scientific—with "scientific" often a code word for being overly skeptical on religious or metaphysical matters. Then, as we get older, we discover that many of the ideas and thought forms in our culture are not only skeptical, they are downright cynical. The dominant philosophies in our colleges and universities are existentialism and deconstruction—both of which often seem to say life is ultimately meaningless. The skeptical mind views people who yearn for a world with greater peace or love or harmony as silly or naive.

Fortunately, we know from the testimony of mystics through the ages that the skeptical or cynical way of seeing things is not the only way. We do not have to be constricted by the negative, pessimistic world view of others. We can believe in the experience of our own ecstasy, and we can choose to live our entire life around the belief that such ecstasy comes from the Sacred and is evidence of a higher way of living and being. We have been born with the capacity to dream and to hope for better things. The way of the mystic is the way of optimism, the way of daring to go after our dreams.

Choose Hope

Remember Pandora? She opened a box created by the Gods, thereby unleashing all sorts of calamities into the world: disease, crime, natural disasters, and so forth. Evils and sorrows ravaged the land, destroying the idyllic paradise that humankind had enjoyed. At the bottom of her box, though, Pandora found hope. Pandora's message: When faced with whatever challenge or obstacle or disaster that may befall you, always respond with hope.

Hope lies at the core of positive thinking—the affirmation that things will get better, even if on the face of it everything seems dark and gloomy. To hope means to offer faith and spiritual devotion to the power of the Sacred. Hope says, in effect, "I refuse to give in to how miserable things appear. I trust that every story, including my own, has a happy ending, for everything exists in the shimmering radiance of Divine presence."

Mysticism invites us to hold fast to our hopes and our dreams. Rather than give in to the social conditioning that things are bad and sure to get worse, mysticism encourages us to believe in our dreams and to respond to the events in our life within the framework of hope. Doing so not only feels good, it empowers us to keep working to actually alleviate suffering and make this world a better place.

Practical Step: *In your journal, set aside a section for writing down your dreams. These could be personal dreams and hopes, as well as aspirations you may have for others or even for all of humanity. Write them down, and hold them sacred. They are your manifestation of hope.*

Stay Humble

When we acknowledge our hopes and dreams and desires for "something more" spiritually, we run into one of the chief dangers of the spiritual life. This danger will walk alongside us the entire length of the mystical way. It is the danger of arrogant pride. This danger tempts us into believing "my dreams are better than those of most people, so I must be better than most people." Or perhaps "I'm a spiritual person, therefore I am better than those thick-headed, selfish materialists who only care about their bank accounts." This is a common, but serious, mistake that aspiring mystics and other spiritual seekers make. We need to avoid this kind of holier-than-thou thinking, for it can undermine the true power of the mystic way.

Mystics truly are out-of-the-ordinary people. We dream dreams, experience visions, and create great masterworks of art, music, and literature. We are the metaphysical nonconformists who never fully fit in. Mystics stand apart from the majority of spiritually minded people who seem content to simply go once a week to church or synagogue or wherever their religion meets, listen to the words of their spiritual leaders, say their prayers, make a financial contribution, and then go back to the mundane business of living. By contrast, mystical seekers never feel fully satisfied with the routine of conventional religion, but rather always yearn for something more—a deeper, more intense, more heartfelt spiritual experience.

There is nothing wrong with either path—the ordinary way or the mystical way.

Each path is appropriate for a certain personality type. Just because you are called to walk one path, it does not make the other path "wrong." This is an important point to remember. Just because there are many different ways of approaching spirituality, does not mean that only one way is right and the others are wrong. Psychologists like Carl Jung have shown that many different types of personalities may be found among different people; certainly there are at least as many spirituality types as there are personality types.

Still, someone with a call to a deep interior spirituality might feel justified in putting down religious behavior that seems so shallow, mundane, and conventional. It's a great temptation to look at the millions of ordinary churchgoers and think, "How can they claim to be spiritual? They just go through the motions of being religious. They cling to rigid beliefs, with never an original thought for themselves. Humph! That's not being spiritual—it's being a sheep!" The aspiring mystic runs the risk of thinking she is an extraordinary person, called by the Sacred to live a special, maybe even enlightened, life. In a way, that's true. But it's true for *all* people, for in the eyes of the Sacred everyone is special, even the ones whose lives are perfectly ordinary and who are comfortable with conventional religion—or even with no religion or spirituality at all. As an aspiring mystic, you have been called onto a wonderful and unusual path, a path few people will walk. But you are no better or wiser or more spiritual than anyone else, especially not in the eyes of the universe. As a wise guy once said, "You are unique, just like everyone else." The path of mystical spirituality is a unique path—it is different, but different does not mean "better than."

Another temptation can arise from this difference between ordinary people and mystical people. It's tempting to decide that because you're the one who's different, then something's wrong with *you*. This is still a put-down, only instead of knocking everyone else, you're putting yourself down. Many spiritual seekers make this mistake, confusing it for humility and thinking it's a great virtue. "Oh, I'm nothing; my needs and wants are not important; don't mind me." But this is not true humility—it's just a put-down; and a put-down is a put-down, whether it is aimed at someone else or at yourself. Either way, it's simply not useful. The Sacred is the source of love and joy and peace—not the source of one-upmanship or put-downs.

Instead of the arrogance of putting others down and the false humility of putting yourself down, the way of the mystic is the way of true humility. But what is humility? It comes from the Latin word *humus*, which means "of the earth." Stated very simply, to be humble is to be down-to-earth. It's as simple as being yourself without the need to judge anyone. Humility involves investing our energies into pursuits more interesting than the dramas of our own egos. If we want to walk the mystic path, we need to admit (at least to ourselves) our spiritual desires, our hopes and dreams. That is the humble thing to do. But then we need to let go of the temptation to start thinking in terms of "how special I am" or "how chosen." Thoughts like that erode the lovely simplicity of humble self-awareness.

Notice how I am choosing to describe the alternative to humility as *arrogance* rather than the traditional idea of *pride*. In the traditional language of mysticism, pride refers to the puffed-up ego, which can be a major stumbling block to spiritual growth. Nowadays, however, pride is often used as a synonym for self-respect, as in "gay pride," which really means gay self-respect. The spiritual view of pride as a problem should not be seen as a criticism of self-respect. A person may be humble (down-to-earth) and self-respecting at the same time. In fact, I don't think you can be humble unless you are self-respecting, since the lack of self-respect is a put-down, and therefore a form of inverted arrogance! Aspiring mystics accept themselves as they are, and in doing so learn to respect and honor all people—even those who may not share their mystical aspirations.

Chapter 3 # Healing the Wounds

Often, we are spurred to explore spirituality and mysticism because of some deep way in which we are unsatisfied with our lives. We may feel life has no meaning, or is over-burdened with hardship and suffering, or we may simply feel that something-is-missing feeling I alluded to earlier. There's nothing wrong with this. After all, we are creatures of desire and longing. As intelligent beings, we know what it is to suffer, and we all live with the knowledge that someday we will die. We know we can and probably will suffer, and so we want ways to overcome the pain. We want to alleviate the hurt and maximize our sense of meaning, joy, and well-being.

In addition to the innate desires and longings we all feel, many of us are wounded—that is to say, we carry the scars and painful memories of the blows we have received over the course of life. For some, these wounds are truly traumatic—some of us are survivors of incest or rape or other forms of abuse, or we are handicapped or otherwise challenged in some significant mental or physical way. For others, the wound may be less horrific, but still painful. Such wounds might include the experience of being emotionally neglected by our families, having religious leaders and school authorities crush our natural curiosity and ability to think for ourselves by insisting we accept their dogmas and comply with their way of doing things, or going through a painful loss, such as a divorce or the death of a loved one.

True mysticism honors the wounds and the longings most of us carry in our hearts and souls. Although this may seem paradoxical, I believe we should celebrate our wounds—for it is often our wounds and our longings that invite us to explore the mystical dimension of life. A wound is an opening up—literally an opening of the flesh, of course; but spiritually speaking a "wound" is anything that opens our spirits to the presence of the Sacred. Many people may never give the spiritual realm of life a second thought, were it not for some way in which their lives experienced suffering or pain. It's almost a cliché that the recovering alcoholic or other addict often makes the transition from substance abuse to spiritual awakening. For many others, the transformation may be less dramatic, but no less real. We often find the door to spirituality through the woundedness in our hearts.

One of my wounds involves my wife and my stepdaughter. Fran, my wife, gave birth to Rhiannon, and almost lost her immediately—for Rhiannon was born with polycystic kidney disease, with several complications including badly underdeveloped lungs. Against all odds (and aided by prayer), Rhiannon survived, even though the doctors thought she wouldn't make it 72 hours. Her first few years were spent in and out of the hospital, as she battled problems with her bowels and blood pressure.

When she was three, Rhiannon suffered a severe stroke that left her paralyzed on her right side. Today, 10 years later, she is confined to a wheelchair and needs assistance in all the basic functions of life—toileting, bathing, getting dressed, and eating. While she is a bright child, the stroke impaired her vision so badly, not to mention the motor skills in her hands, that learning has come very slowly, and she finds reading difficult and writing impossible without a computer—and even then, her achievement moves at a snail's pace.

My wound, of course, is tiny compared to Rhiannon's, and much smaller than Fran's. Fran's wound is the recognition that her own daughter is leading a life of chronic and overwhelming suffering and anger, and the frustration that comes with realizing she cannot change Rhiannon's situation. My wound is simply an ongoing recognition that I am powerless to alleviate the suffering of those I love, and I must simply accept that powerlessness on a daily basis. Mine is the smallest of the three—but I know how painful mine is, so I can only imagine the suffering Rhiannon and Fran endure.

I scream to the gods, asking why such a terrible handicap is even possible in our world—what good does it serve? Why must Rhiannon—and by extension, Fran and I—be burdened by this debilitating medical condition? How do we make sense out of this? Where do we find the strength to keep caring for Rhiannon, and keep encouraging her to grow to the best of her ability?

No simple answers, of course. But all three of us know that our life is not meaningless. Fran and I see in Rhiannon a powerful resilience and sense of humor and delight in life. We witness small miracles—right now, as a teenager, Rhiannon is finally learning how to read—and are regularly heartened by the kindness of both strangers and loved ones. Most of all, we see in Rhiannon the fierce way in which life refuses to just surrender in the face of pain and suffering. And in that, we see echoes of the Sacred, of the Source of all life and light and love. So, in all her heartbreaking limitations, Rhiannon has become a doorway through which we all encounter the Sacred.

Aspiring mystics are called to befriend our wounds. Thanks to my wounds, I know we can find God even through (and perhaps especially through) the ways in which we have been broken and beaten by life. Get to know your wounds, and look for evidence of miracles around them.

Wounded, But Not Victimized

Acknowledging and even embracing the ways in which our lives are broken, wounded, or otherwise unsatisfactory can be truly liberating. We live in a culture that seems so committed to pretending everything is okay, that we are strong and capable and never afraid or otherwise troubled. Wear a mask, hide your true feelings, and keep a stiff upper lip. In this culture of false confidence, it's a relief to simply say, "No, I'm not perfect; yes, I have deep areas of dissatisfaction and unresolved pain in my life." However, there is a danger in acknowledging and accepting our broken parts.

The danger is that we can actually fall in love with our wounds, and let our brokenness control our lives. Odd as it may sound, it can actually be a lot of fun to be wounded. When we're wounded, people who love us take extra special care of us, in hopes of our healing. But we don't always want to be healed—for then we would lose the extra attention, the extra care, and the special privileges that come with being wounded. If we were healed, we'd be normal and ordinary again. In other words, we'd have to accept being treated just like everyone else.

Rhiannon, Fran, and I try to remain mindful that Rhiannon is a person, not a handicap. She is defined by her abilities, not her disabilities. She is more than just her wounds. When working on her homework or her physical therapy, she does not get to use her handicap as an excuse for not trying. By the same token, Fran and I support each other to make sure we don't fall into the "poor me" trap of letting our entire lives be overwhelmed by the stress of caring for a chronically ill child. If we devote energy to feeling sorry for ourselves (or congratulating ourselves for being such saintly parents), we know that we are simply diverting energy away from the more important tasks of caring for Rhiannon—and for ourselves.

Here is where the mystic way proves vitally important. For us, and I suspect for anyone who is in the process of healing a wound, whether it is a physical or a spiritual wound, much energy is required. We know how much our body needs rest after an illness. In the wake of any wound, a person's body and soul needs extra energy to find equilibrium when healing that wound. This is true whether the wound is physical, like Rhiannon's stroke, or emotional, such as getting over the end of a relationship.

Spirituality—our connectedness to the Divine Source—can be an energy pipeline. Think of God as the ultimate power generator in the universe, creating an endless resource of energy in the forms of love and light and joy. When we practice the tools of the aspiring mystic—praying and meditating regularly, spending time in silence, reading sacred scriptures and other useful writings—we are tapping into that energy source. We are allowing the positive energy of the Sacred to enter into us. This energy has two purposes: to provide healing in our own lives, and then to be a resource we can tap into as we love and support others.

So, when you honor your wounds, the ways big and small in which your life is not how you hope or wish it could be, remember that a key element of the mystical life is healing. You will ultimately be asked to sacrifice your wound—to give it to the gods. Maybe you'll be like Rhiannon, who probably won't fully give up her wounds until she physically dies. Or you may be asked to accept healing right here and right now. Either way, as you progress in the mystical life, you will receive healing energy, and you will be expected to use that energy positively, both in your own healing and in helping others heal.

Be Positive

No matter how healthy or how wounded we are, no matter how spiritually advanced or how humble we are, no matter what circumstances our life may have given us—the path of the mystic calls for a positive and hopeful approach.

No matter how much we pretend to be happy, strong, perfectly well-adjusted beings, the fact is that everyone's life has some level of dissatisfaction or some form of brokenness. Out of this shadow side of our wounds and our unsatisfied longings, we each face the temptation to become negative, cynical, and bitter. We can decide life is a lousy affair. We can say everything stinks and who cares? Then we can go open another beer or light another cigarette and just sit and watch reruns on the TV.

Thankfully, most people who are attracted to the mystical path have not succumbed to such extreme levels of bitterness. Even when we drink beer and watch TV, we tend to do so in moderation! It's difficult to pursue mysticism and cynicism at the same time, because mysticism is the ultimate alternative of cynicism. Mysticism is built on hope—the hope that the Sacred not only exists, but is intimately available to each one of us, as a source of love and healing and ecstasy.

So when I say, "be positive," I probably don't have to tell those of you who are reading this to give up such extreme negative cynicism. Sadly, too many people in our world have surrendered themselves to bitter negativity—but persons who have chosen cynicism as their god probably would not bother to read this book! But even though mystically oriented people usually are more positive than negative, most of us still have plenty of room to grow when it comes to cultivating a positive approach to ourselves, to others, and to the Sacred.

Many aspiring mystics tend to keep their negative thoughts focused on themselves. "I'm not worthy of God." "I'm a misfit." "I never do anything right." "I'm a failure at life." "I think I'm going crazy." Thoughts like these are not just the problem of spiritual seekers, but they certainly plague many of us. Often, people trapped in the vise of negative thought patterns don't even realize this is going on. It seems that such thoughts lurk just below the level of conscious awareness, but they color the way we view life and understand our relationships.

The way of the mystic is the way of love, as surely as it is the way of wonder and ecstasy. My encounter with the Sacred that I described in Chapter 1 was essentially an encounter with love.

You Gotta Believe

Central to the mystical life is the ability to believe.

Belief is not the same thing as "absolute certainty" or "lack of doubt." Authentic belief involves an open-hearted, love-oriented willingness to accept and relate to whatever it is we believe in. To believe in God does not mean you have proof positive that God exists. No one has such a thing. Believing in God means you're willing to take a chance on God, to open your heart in love and trust to the source of all life and light and creation.

Affirmations and positive thoughts are a way of believing in yourself. When you make an affirming statement about yourself (such as, "I now attract the ideal job into my life") it's not just a bunch of New Age hooey. Rather, it's a statement of belief—of being willing to take a chance on the good outcome, the happy ending, on things working out for the best.

When we take the time to think positive thoughts in a disciplined way, we are training our mind to operate according to principles of love and joy—characteristics of the Divine. Positive thoughts feel good, and keep us open to new possibilities, unexpected miracles, and emerging opportunities. If you want to learn more about affirmations and their potential for transforming your life, consult the writings of Louise Hay, Florence Scovel Shinn, or Sondra Ray.

Practical Step: *On a regular basis—say, once a month—write a short affirmation that can help you to be more positive, more hopeful, more believing. Something like "God provides me everything I need" or "I trust the universe to provide me guidance." The best affirmations are the ones we have to stretch into; they challenge our doubts with the power of the positive words. Once you create your affirmation, use it regularly, perhaps as a daily mantra before you meditate.*

Julian of Norwich's mystical experience was a revelation of Divine love. Again and again, mystical experiences both large and small convey a quality of love.

Love—whether understood in mystical terms or more down-to-earth ways—is the energy of positive, nurturing relationships. This starts with ourselves; if we believe God loves us, and we believe we are called to be more like God, then we must begin by loving ourselves. And one important way to love ourselves involves patterning the mind to think positive, loving thoughts, rather than critical put-down thoughts. For all the energy we give them, those put-down thoughts are rarely useful. We do better to replace them with thoughts of creativity and love and nurture.

Reprogramming our minds to be positive about ourselves requires being positive about others as well. The way of the mystic calls us to manifest love both inward (toward ourselves) and outward (toward others). Who do you have difficulty loving? Your mother-in-law? Your boss? The neighbor with the loud dogs? This applies not only to individuals, but to entire groups as well. Do you find it difficult to love gay people? Republicans? Born-again Christians? Liberals? Racists? People of color? Time after time, each of us will encounter individual persons, or entire groups, for whom we feel little or no love. I know as an aspiring mystic I must sacrifice my negative thoughts (stereotypes) about other people, whether it's a group of people or a certain individual, for whom I lack positive regard. Why is this important? Because one of the ways in which I love myself better is by loving others better, especially those with whom I disagree or whose behavior I disapprove of. Of course, loving a person is not the same as condoning objectionable behavior. But if I want to help someone improve his or her negative behavior, first I must be very clear about loving that person.

Hand in hand with learning to be positive about ourselves and positive about others is the call to be positive in our thoughts about, and toward, the Sacred. To be an aspiring mystic means to adopt a spirit of openness and love toward that which is beyond all names. Aspire to love the source of love—for that will be your energy source as you endeavor to be more loving toward yourself and toward others. It also means being willing to challenge the negative ideas about the Sacred that you may have learned growing up. Were you taught that God is wrathful? Or that the universe doesn't care about you? Do you harbor a secret thought about the Sacred that suggests God is unfair, or indifferent, or abusive? Such ideas will simply hold you back as you seek to find your Divine bliss. Calling God wrathful is like calling yourself worthless—it's not only inaccurate, but it serves to extinguish love. Choose to think about the Infinite in positive ways. It's necessary for fostering a deeper relatedness to the Divine.

No Denial

The quest to develop more positive thought forms (and consequently, behavior) needs to be an honest quest. In other words, we need to be positive, but we also need to be honest about the negative realities of our world. A positive mystic doesn't pretend that death, suffering, injustice, and abuse do not exist—nor does he pretend that such things are spiritually unimportant. Likewise, aspiring mystics do not deny their own mortality, or those parts of themselves they don't like (such as rage, jealousy, doubt, or fear). Denial does not help a person become more loving and more positive. In fact, just the opposite is true—denial can hinder us from growing and maturing on the mystical way.

Why is this? Because denial is fundamentally dishonest. Love is positive, but love is also real. Love does not pretend everything is perfect. The positive nature of love arises out of trust that no matter how bad things are, they can and will get better. Love provides the energy of healing—meaning, of course, that sometimes healing is necessary. This is true in both our inner and outer universes. For example, our negative thoughts—the thoughts by which we put ourselves and others down—often signify the places in our souls where we need healing. Our prejudices and resentments toward others also represent those places that need healing. And our tendencies to act out our negative thoughts in abusive or neglectful behaviors mark the need for healing as well.

In the external world, many huge problems exist that need healing. Our society struggles with the burden of economic inequities, often connected to problems like racism and sexism. Terrible crime and addiction plague our inner cities, areas rooted in poverty and despair. Spiritual people sometimes blame poverty on the poor themselves ("We create our own reality. If the poor would only choose abundance, they would have it!"), but such blaming is both unhelpful and unfair. Very few poor people want to be poor. And even if the minds of poor persons are filled with negative thought patterns holding them back, they equally suffer from a lack of opportunities to truly advance themselves out of their impoverished state.

How uncomfortable we feel about acknowledging our wounds! We don't want to see business executives cry after a bad day on Wall Street, or military leaders sob when young men die in combat. No, the code in our society is "stuff your negative feelings, and put on a happy face toward the world." We need to learn, not only as individuals but as a society, how to acknowledge the dark side of things—whether it's the dark of our wounds, or the dark of the many negative thoughts and circumstances currently manifest in our world. Once we acknowledge our wounds, our negativity, and our personal and social problems, then we've taken the first step toward healing.

As an aspiring mystic, don't deny the negative. There's no use pretending that negative thoughts or sickness or suffering don't exist. There's certainly no use thinking the suffering of others is only their own fault. On the contrary, be honest and real about the places that need healing. After all, the mystical life calls us to nurture love and healing. It's not only the life of gee-whiz experiences, but a life of transformation and of helping to create a better world. Choose love and positive energy, and remember that such a choice calls you to be a force for healing—and not just for yourself. We are all interconnected; our behaviors and thoughts impact others as much as they impact ourselves.

Mystical Realism

All of the seemingly unrelated topics we've covered so far—from acknowledging our capacity for ecstasy and wonder to accepting our desires and our dreams for spiritual enlightenment; from learning to be humble to being willing to honor and perhaps even celebrate our wounds—all these elements point to the same end: the willingness to accept ourselves just as we are. This is essential to progress in the spiritual life. When we learn how important honest self-acceptance is to the spiritual quest, then we've reached a place I call "mystical realism."

For most of us, this means accepting ourselves as imperfect creatures—creatures yet to become all we would like ourselves to be. Mystical realism means accepting our noblest and highest aspirations, and also accepting what some psychologists call the shadow—that part of ourselves dominated by fear, jealousy, rage, or other feelings we might secretly wish weren't there. This is not easy for any of us to do—especially living in a society that practically worships the idols of perfection, mastery, achievement, and control.

It's not good enough to just "be yourself" in our society. You have to *do* something, make a difference, perform a function, master a skill, achieve greatness, in order to be noticed or to count for something. A person is considered worthy not by who she is, but by what she does. And our society, as a whole, often wants the shadow to just go away. We want convicted felons to be put to death and we want the homeless and mentally ill to be swept off our streets. We fear the shadow, and so it remains unhealed on a societal level, just as it remains unhealed among many of us as individuals.

The realism of self-acceptance is critical to the mystical life, for mysticism runs counter to our society's idolatry of achievement and perfection. Society wants every person to perform—to perform great achievements, or at least to perform some sort of job or task with flawless perfection. But instead of emphasizing *performance*, mysticism emphasizes *relationship*. A mystic is someone who enjoys a personal, intimate relationship with the Source of all mystery. We do not have to perform anything to be a mystic. We simply need to accept who we are, exercise our capacity for wonder, and be aware of the miracles in our lives.

Consider this common theme in stories and folklore: a man meets a woman he likes, and immediately worries that he's not good enough for her. Therefore, he proceeds to do all sorts of things to impress her, acting as if he is somehow wealthier, or more powerful, or more intelligent, or whatever, than he really is—only to find out, usually to his chagrin, that all she really wants is for him to be himself. She doesn't need him to pretend to be something he's not—really, she wants just the opposite. She wants him to accept himself as he is, with all his foibles and limitations.

Relating to the Great Mystery works in much the same way. One temptation many spiritual beginners face is the temptation to spiritual performance. It works like this: A person can pretend to be a "great psychic" or "enlightened mystic" or whatever, often to impress other people but maybe even out of a secret belief that this is necessary to impress God. It arises from the idea that we need to perform a certain way in order to be a spiritual master. Alas, such spiritual arrogance does nothing to impress the angels or the gods. Likewise, it's easy to say "I am God" or "I create my own reality"— and while both of those statements might contain a kernel of truth insofar as the Sacred and the forces of creativity are manifest in all beings, ultimately such grandiose one-sided statements ring hollow. After all, it is as equally true (but less glamorous) to say "I am mortal" and "my creativity is limited by forces beyond my control." Pretending to be more spiritually powerful or metaphysically advanced than we really are will do little more than annoy the other human beings who have to deal with us on a day-by-day basis.

Here's the good news for aspiring mystics: The Source of all the wonder and ecstasy in the world does not need us to prove anything. The Heart of the Mystery is not worried about whether or not you or I ever measure up to anything. If anything, all that God wants from you is a willingness to be loving, open, compassionate, and caring—and humble.

"Ah," you may be thinking, "but what about believing in my dream? What about my desire to be filled with God's presence on an ongoing basis, or to be empowered with spiritual ecstasy flowing through my body? Ultimately, I really *do* want to be more than what I am—much more!"

Fair enough. It's part of the human condition to want more than what we have, and I would much rather see people desire more spiritual enlightenment than just more consumer goods. However, in our quest to attain the joy of mystical union with the Divine, we need to start at the beginning, which means humbly accepting where we are. Mystical realism. And then the next, perhaps even harder, fact to accept is that we probably won't reach our spiritual goals as quickly or as effortlessly as we'd like.

It's tempting to think of mysticism almost as the spiritual equivalent of the Olympics. It's wonderful to watch an Olympic athlete perform on television, in front of millions and millions of adoring fans. Maybe being a mystic would be just like that—the mystic delivers a flawless spiritual performance, meditating her way into pure Divine consciousness, and then takes a bow while receiving the applause of the angels, smiling as she receives wave after wave of perfect Divine bliss.

Maybe for some mystics—of the caliber of Julian of Norwich or Francis of Assisi—this would be an appropriate analogy. But for most of us, the spiritual life is nothing like the Olympics. Or, at the very least, not without years and years of excruciating, difficult practice. If Olympic athletes have to put in years and years of dedicated hard work to earn their gold medals, why should we be any different as we embark on the spiritual quest? And even after all those years of practice, very few athletes make it to the Olympics. Fortunately for most of us, it is not necessary to perform in the Olympics to enjoy the accomplishment and satisfaction that comes from being a powerful athlete. We can enjoy the pleasure of sports without having to perform in world-renowned competitions. Well, spirituality works much the same way.

Dedication and committed effort are essential for every seeker on the spiritual path, but it's a mistake to think of this quest only in terms of success or achievement. You do not have to be a "spiritual Olympian" in order to be acceptable to the Sacred. And even if you eventually do reach the heights that were scaled by Francis of Assisi or Julian of Norwich, the first goal on your journey is learning how to be an everyday mystic—someone whose life is filled with ordinary miracles and quiet wonders.

Your Soul Is Bigger Than Your Body

The path of the mystic is the path of nurturing the soul. One of the central mysteries of life is the mystery of the soul, which could be defined as the totality of a person's being. Wondrous and unfathomable, a person's soul consists of body, mind, and spirit, yet somehow more than just the sum of its parts. Since being a mystic means being an explorer of life's mysteries, then a mystic is a person who explores—and nurtures, and celebrates—his or her soul.

I like to think of a mystic as an athlete of the soul. Athletes explore the possibilities and the abilities of the human body. By pushing her body to its limit, through exercise, practice, and competition, an athlete can discover strength she never imagined she possessed. She can discover a sense of joy not only in winning, but even more fundamentally in simply doing her best. In a similar way, the exercises and practices an aspiring mystic performs help to develop her "spiritual fitness." When you walk the path of the mystic, your competition will not be with members of another team, but rather with your own self. You will compete with that part of yourself which would rather not bother with the hard work of loving. You will compete with that aspect of yourself which believes you should hate or reject or deny parts of yourself. You will compete with that aspect of yourself which considers mysticism and spirituality to be a waste of time because it isn't practical or profitable. You will compete with your own fears—with that part of yourself which is afraid of life, afraid of love, afraid of creativity and healing and transformation.

Mystics from centuries past called this soul-level competition "spiritual warfare," and labeled the fearful and negative and unloving parts of the soul as "demons." Such strong language doesn't seem very useful for today's aspiring mystics. One of the challenges of entering into the mysteries of the soul is learning to love, accept, and transform our shadow side, rather than rejecting it as demonic.

The great mystical traditions regard the soul as infinitely larger than the body. Your soul is not contained within your body, but rather your body exists within your soul. Your soul is not limited by space, or time, or matter. In a nanosecond, your soul can travel from the mundane world of the five senses, into the infinite glories and majestic wonders of the very heart of God. And just as quickly, the soul can bring the Sacred fully back into your body, transforming your entire self into a sudden, shimmering recognition of eternity, right here and right now. Think of your soul as the bridge that links your body and your mind to the very heart of the gods themselves. Nothing separates the mind of God from the ground of your soul, and so your soul is the bridge linking your limited awareness with the realities of the Infinite. As an aspiring mystic, you are declaring to the universe that you desire to cross that bridge.

To explore the landscape of your soul requires the use of your imagination. Imagination opens the doorway to the unlimited wealth of images, sensations, ideas, and feelings that make up the data banks of your soul. While your body is limited by the laws of space and time, the imaginary capacities of your soul have no boundaries. When you imagine yourself basking in the presence of the Sacred, or aflame with the passionate vision of the Goddess, you open your soul to the possibilities of mystical experience—experience that can come unbidden, in ways even more powerful and vivid than the most intense mental image.

But I don't mean to suggest the inner work of your mystic is "just your imagination," meaning somehow unreal or unreliable. We can easily explain away any and every mystical experience, no matter how powerful, as nothing more than a psychological mind game. Even the world-shattering experiences of Jesus, the Buddha, and all the other saints and mystics who ever lived could be discounted as mere psychological fireworks. This is the self-righteous position of the skeptical rationalist, who hides behind a cloak of scientific rationalism to discount any and all spiritual phenomena. Alas for those who take such a position, for they will miss out on the possibilities of a lifetime—the possibilities of crossing that soul-bridge to the Sacred, and transforming your life in the service of healing and love and joy.

Far from succumbing to the pessimism of the skeptic, great mystics have tended to see imagination not as a child's realm of make-believe, but rather as the threshold to an infinite world of love and possibility. Consider the wisdom of William Blake: "What is now proved was once only imagin'd" and "Every thing possible to be believ'd is an image of truth." So trust your imagination. It is more real than you think—more real than our weary and cynical culture wants us to think. By exploring the limitless world of your imagination and soul, you gradually empower yourself to make concrete changes in your life in the "real world" of matter. Just like Jesus could heal the sick or the Buddha could transmit enlightenment, the spiritual potential of mysticism is more than just a head trip—it can and will revolutionize your outer life as much as it transforms your inner life. But it begins on the inside. What will someday be proven is now only imagined.

Honor Your Body

By saying the soul is larger than the body, I run a great risk—the risk of implying that the soul is somehow more important or more holy than the body. Spiritual seekers often think this way, for this idea has bedeviled religions and mystical traditions the world over. If you are harboring any thoughts along those lines, let go of them now. Just because the soul is larger than the body does not make it more important, more holy, or more God-like. Just because the soul is the bridge to mystical union does not give it a higher value than our material dimension. On the contrary, true spirituality recognizes that Divine presence exists everywhere. God is omnipresent, which is to say in all places at all times. This means that God resides as fully in the human body as in the human soul.

Naturally, the body can get sick, can be wounded, and eventually dies. For these reasons, many people have viewed the spiritual quest as a way to escape the limitations of the body and find refuge in the immortality of the soul. But as soon as we decide the body is lower than the soul, then we have an excuse to neglect the body and to reject such body-oriented things as sexuality or powerful emotions. Such neglect and self-rejection can actually undermine our progress on the mystic way—remember, mysticism is about love and healing, not contempt or self-negation. Rejecting any part of ourselves—even a "lower" part—means to reject something that rests within the omnipresence of the Divine.

Earlier I suggested that, as spiritual athletes, we compete with that aspect of ourselves that wants to reject our lower or unspiritual parts. One of the easiest ways for aspiring mystics to reject parts of themselves is by hating or neglecting their bodies. Hatred is hatred, which means it stands opposed to the way of mystical love. Even mild forms of hatred (like neglect, or excessively stern discipline) prove inconsistent with the ways of the Sacred, which are the ways of love.

Despite the body's limitations, we need to love it—if for no other reason than because we need to practice our ability to love. While it's easy to love someone or something that is strong and beautiful and powerful, often we resist loving someone or something that is vulnerable and weak and limited. In spiritual terms: it's easy to love the soul, for it has a powerful imagination, endless ability to love and care for others, and is immortal in its connectedness to the Divine. But sometimes it's harder to love the body, which is not only clumsy and limited but after all will eventually die, and will probably suffer many wounds or illnesses between now and death. And yet, when we love our body—by getting enough rest, exercise, eating a healthy diet, and enjoying sexuality in appropriate ways—we sharpen our mind and our awareness, tools that will help us bring a more keen awareness and knowing to the task of finding God.

Mysticism may be primarily an exercise of the soul, but at least on this side of death, the soul remains grounded in the body. Even the word ecstasy—which literally means "out of the place

Exercise, Diet, Rest, Sleep

Loving and caring for your physical body is not an optional duty. The soul needs a healthy body as much as the body needs a healthy soul. Here are four fundamental principles to loving your body:

1. **Diet.** *Focus on fresh fruits, vegetables, and whole grains. Moderate amounts of sugars, fats, or alcohol may be appropriate, but beware of any of these foods when you have a habit of overdoing them.*

2. **Exercise.** *Your unique circumstances will determine what kind of a program is right for you. For many people, a 30-minute workout three times a week can provide tremendous benefit.*

3. **Sleep.** *Ours is a sleep-deprived culture. Are you often fatigued, irritable, or unproductive? Catching up on your shuteye may be what you need.*

4. **Rest.** *In addition to sleep, it's important to observe the sabbath (one full day of rest each week) as well as vacation or retreat time on a regular basis. Give your body down time.*

Refer to your physician, counselor, or other health care professional for designing a diet or exercise program that's right for you. Just be sure to take the time to lovingly care for your body. Caring for your body means caring for yourself.

Practical Step: *Pick one of these four areas in which you would like to make constructive change. Make a plan. Join Weight Watchers, or a fitness club. Rearrange your schedule to get eight hours of sleep. Plan a real vacation, where you'll do nothing but lie on the beach for a week. And do it. To make sure you follow through, include a trusted friend in your plans to help you stay accountable.*

you stand"—suggests that mysticism involves a moving out *from the body*. In the spiritual life, the body serves the soul the same way that a tree's roots serves the trunk and leaves that reach with yearning to the sun. Deny your body, and you are no healthier than a tree with cut-off roots. But when you love your body, you love your soul—and vice versa. Don't reject or neglect either one.

Practice . . .

Becoming a mystic involves a process similar to becoming a millionaire. Our culture abounds with advertisements and opportunities for getting rich with little or no effort. In the back of magazines, in junk mail, and spam e-mail, we encounter countless announcements of yet another get-rich-quick scheme. It's beguiling to think that, for little more than the price of a lottery ticket, or a high-powered seminar by a fast-talking human-potential guru, or an information packet ordered through the Internet, you could soon be on easy street. But any financial counselor—or anyone with more than a lick of common sense—will point out that the real way to get rich is by a slow and sure plan of managing your money, curbing your spending, and investing wisely. It almost never happens overnight. Sure, one person wins the lottery, but millions more are simply out of a dollar—or many dollars. So rather than pinning your hopes on a one-in-a-million chance, it simply makes more sense wisely and carefully to manage your money.

It's the same way with an athlete: a slow and steady regimen of practice, practice, practice is the price of admission to the Olympics. The winning Olympian and the successful millionaire have an important quality they share—a crucial quality the aspiring mystic needs to cultivate: *They both love the process as much as the goal.* In other words, to become a successful athlete, you must love the process of slowly improving your skill as much as you love the thrill of victory. To become a millionaire, you must love the gradual process of making deals, investing your cash, and watching your wealth grow, at least as much as you would love buying that mansion in Palm Beach.

Spirituality works the same way. If all you want is to be a mystical superstar, in which you effortlessly glide through life with a sense of God as your co-pilot . . . well, I'm afraid I can't help you. And I'd be really suspicious of anyone who claims they can.

It's important to love the process of *becoming* a mystic. Love the gradual transformation as you take the journey from mundane to mystical. If it seems that it takes forever, remember that great mystics like Julian of Norwich or Teresa of Avila spent literally years—or even decades—in disciplined prayer and meditation before they were rewarded with their visions or ecstasies. Keep in mind that anything which comes cheap probably has little or no lasting value. The experience of merging into unitive Oneness with the Sacred is the most valuable experience anyone can ever have, therefore it will not come cheaply.

Granted, for a tiny minority of people the experience of mystical awareness may seem as effortless as buying a winning lottery ticket. But no one will ever fully understand how another person attains spiritual transformation, so we need to let go of the temptation to compare ourselves with others. For most of us the mystical journey can be summed up in the old proverb: Practice makes perfect. And even if we never attain perfection—in other words, never become the mystical equivalent of an Olympic athlete—if we perform the spiritual exercises of the aspiring mystic with love and devotion, we will soon learn that it doesn't matter how much we achieve, for what really matters is the love and devotion that will fill our hearts and minds with radiance and splendor.

But what are the "spiritual exercises" of the aspiring mystic? Read on. We've looked at the raw material of the spiritual life:

Maintaining a positive attitude, fostering the imagination, acknowledging both the ecstasy and the wounds of life. Now it is time to begin shaping that material into a disciplined practice of opening our hearts, minds, and souls to God. This discipline includes such actions as forming healthy relationships and caring for others, cultivating a practice of silence and meditation, learning to find balance between work and play, meditation and dance, silence and celebration...these are the tasks that you, as an aspiring mystic, are called to undertake. As you endeavor to master these mystical "tools of the trade," you are no more guaranteed a pure vision of God than the budding athlete is guaranteed a place on the Olympic team. But you *are* guaranteed a life centered on love and devotion in relationship to the Sacred, a life where the ordinary *moments* of life are gradually transformed into the ordinary *miracles* of life. And the mystics who have gone before us report that even this humble mysticism has its share of wonder and ecstasy—and it is reward enough.

Chapter 4 Knowing What You Want

My daughter leaves for school every morning at 6:30 A.M. While a part of me thinks that is an obscenely early time to be up—not only for children, but for grownups too—I mostly am thankful for our schedule. Fran and I can focus on helping Rhiannon get up, get dressed, get in her wheelchair and out the door to meet her bus; then after she leaves we have a window of opportunity for our morning spiritual exercises before our days begin in earnest.

We've set aside part of a room for a small home shrine. A small coffee table, handmade by Fran's father almost 50 years ago, serves as our little altar. It's draped with a beautiful deep blue cloth accented with gold stars. We intentionally keep the tabletop as uncluttered as possible. We have a statue of the Buddha on one side, with a statue of Gaia—Mother Earth—on the other. In front of them are symbols of the four elements: an incense burner representing air, a candle signifying fire, a handmade clay bowl filled with water, and a large quartz crystal for earth. On the left front corner of the altar is an hourglass, and on the opposite side a Tibetan bell—symbols of time and eternity, respectively. Behind the altar hangs a colorful icon of Jesus cradled in the arms of his mother Mary. In front of the altar, on the floor, we've placed two zabutons and zafus—cushions, originally designed by Zen monks, for sitting on while meditating.

Our morning routine—or ritual, if you will—is very simple. We reverently bow before the altar, as a way of offering devotion to the Sacred Presence whom we believe is represented by the Buddha, by Christ and Mary, and by the Goddess Gaia. We light the candle and burn a stick of incense, thereby honoring the elements, which not only symbolize the physical nature of our world, but also the physicality of our bodies. Then whoever happens to be sitting on the right rings the bell, while the other one turns the hourglass. (Although recently, we've taken to using a small battery-powered kitchen timer instead. Silent as it is, an hourglass is distracting since it needs to be watched to see when time is up, whereas the timer quietly beeps for us. We are aspiring mystics who tend toward the practical.) As the tone of the bell slowly reverberates into eternity, we settle into our quiet time—time of prayer, meditation, and consciously offering our souls to the Divine.

I wish I could simply write a rhapsody about the many ecstasies and supernatural joys that manifest about us as we go about our daily practice. Having been a student of meditation for over 15 years now, part of me thinks I ought to be a master of meditative silence. But truth be told, a daily practice of meditation, even after many years, works much the same as any other daily routine. In other words, it has its ups and downs. Some mornings, particularly if I'm facing a deadline or have some other emotional or work-related challenge weighing upon me,

I'm doing well to simply sit and struggle to find my center. My worrisome thoughts assault me like little darts, not very dangerous but certainly no fun, either. On my worst days, I seem to offer up to God only a fidgety faithfulness, squirming like some impatient child eager to crawl out of mommy's lap to go play. On days like that, why do I even bother to sit in the silence? For much the same reason why Fran and I hug and kiss when we meet and part, even if we're in the midst of working through a tough issue that leaves one or both of us feeling less than affectionate. Like marriage, spirituality stretches love out beyond the fickle nature of human feelings, into a larger, more spacious love based on conscious commitment, keeping promises, and honoring both parties in the relationship. When I chose to love Fran and married her, my love graduated from the passionate unruliness of mere emotion into a larger love, which is defined not only by my needs and expectations but by hers as well. So, too, the aspiring mystic at some point needs to make a similar commitment to a relationship with the Infinite. This is why many mystics have described their journey as a spiritual marriage—such as this passage from the prophecies of Isaiah:

> *For as a young man marries a young woman, so shall*
> *your builder marry you, and as the bridegroom rejoices*
> *over the bride, so shall your God rejoice over you.*

Like most mystical poetry, images such as this carry meaning on several levels. On one hand, it suggests that the joy and pleasure of spiritual union may be compared to the ecstasies of sexual intercourse. But on another level, it also points to how the spiritual life embodies many of the same issues and themes of the married life: commitment, partnership, faithfulness, and trust.

So when I'm having a "bad prayer day," I look to my commitment and my trust rather than to my feelings for guidance. I believe it's better for my soul, and a better expression of my devotion to the Divine, to sit there and fidget, rather than to just give up. And even on my most distracted and fidgety days, I usually feel at least somewhat more calm and centered when I take the time to pray and meditate.

But I don't mean to just paint a gloomy picture. Like I said, a daily discipline of prayer and meditation has its ups as well as its downs. Sometimes I am surprised at the ease with which I seem to be ushered in to a sense of God's presence. My prayer seems to flow with an eloquence and emotional honesty I didn't realize I possessed, or my silent meditation seems to quickly and effortlessly open up into a spacious place of relaxed awareness and a sense of deep, abiding peace. Rather than feeling that I have to discipline or reign in my unruly "monkey mind," these graced times of connection with the Sacred seem to sparkle with a focused inner silence. These are moments of true communion, when I feel as if the connection between me and the heart of the universe has been thrown wide open, and God is closer to me than I am to myself.

When I was younger, I believed the object of the mystical life was to cultivate this kind of powerful, graced experience on an ongoing basis. I yearned to have God-consciousness 24-7. Now I'm a bit less demanding in my spiritual goals. I still want to connect with the Divine as often and as fully as possible, but I no longer expect it to be a constant ecstasy. It would be like the sun always shining, or the season always being summer. We need nighttime, darkness, and winter. The soul needs a break from the pleasures of Divine awareness. It's okay to have times of "desolation" as well as "consolation" (those are the words that mystics in sixteenth-century Spain used to describe the experience of God's absence or God's presence).

So every morning we ring the bell again, set the timer, and enter into the silence. The grand rhythms of eternity and the universe are suddenly held in the open palms resting in our laps. Sometimes it's a frustrating exercise in fidgety faith, and other times it's a morning radiant with a shimmering sense of the Holy. Each morning is a new adventure.

Then the timer beeps (or the hourglass runs out of sand). We get up, take our showers, dress, and eat; then we're off to another day of work and the simple joys of living.

Every Day

Here, then, is the core of mystical practice. Anyone who aspires to live a mystical life needs to pray or meditate, in some form, every day. I'm sorry if this doesn't seem very glamorous, sexy, or exciting, but it's the truth as best I know it. I know there are books out there that promise mystical experiences in 30 days (honest!), but to that kind of spirituality I say: You get what you pay for. Invest 30 days into mysticism, and you'll have an experience worthy of your investment. If you want to have a lifetime's worth of spiritual unfoldment, you'll need to give it your all. Day in and day out. There are no shortcuts to glory, no spiritual equivalent of the lottery.

This doesn't mean your practice will look like mine. Exactly how you understand prayer and meditation will depend largely on your spiritual or religious tradition. Whether you pray, meditate, or do both depends on whether you see the Sacred in personal terms (God, Goddess) or in impersonal terms (the Tao, the Source). Basically, if you approach the Sacred seeking a personal

Study to Meditate

It's better to learn meditation from a teacher, but that's not always possible. And even if you are working with a qualified instructor, it's nice to have a book or two on the subject. Fortunately, some great books from a variety of perspectives are available. Here are a few I've found particularly useful:

The Other Side of Silence *by Morton Kelsey. A Christian approach to meditation.*

How to Meditate *by Lawrence LeShan. Psychological and non-sectarian approach.*

The Relaxation Response *by Herbert Bensen. Stresses the physical benefits of meditation.*

The Cloud of Unknowing *(anonymous). Medieval Christian handbook on contemplative prayer. The fourteenth-century language is very stern, but the insights are astute and timeless.*

Peace Is Every Step *by Thich Nhat Hanh. Vietnamese Buddhist and peace activist teaches mindfulness as a daily practice.*

The Path Is the Goal *by Chögyam Trungpa. One of the foremost teachers of Tibetan Buddhism in the West wrote this short introduction to Buddhist practice.*

Reading about meditation can inspire you to be diligent in your practice. However, there are two traps to avoid. First, don't let your reading about meditation (or prayer) be a substitute for actually doing it. Close the book and practice! Second, don't assume the book will teach you all you need to know. There's still no substitute for a flesh-and-blood teacher.

Practical Step: *Get one of these books, or a similar one that your meditation teacher or some other knowledgeable person might recommend to you. Read it. Write down your thoughts, questions, reflections, and arguments with the book in your journal. Read your meditation book right before or after you meditate. Even if you only read two pages a day, it can be quite helpful.*

relationship, you pray. If you approach the Sacred seeking an impersonal connectedness, you meditate. But aside from that rather simplistic distinction, the difference between prayer and meditation is pretty fuzzy. At least one form of prayer—contemplative prayer—is virtually indistinguishable from many forms of meditation. Meditation and contemplative prayer both involve taking the time to still your mind, quiet your thoughts, and focus on your breathing and your body, so that you may enter into a silent, relaxed state of awareness. Doing so on a daily basis will revolutionize your spirituality.

Perhaps the most effective approach to mysticism would be to combine elements of both meditation and prayer in your daily practice. Prayer, as a way of disclosing our innermost soul to the universe, can be a profoundly moving experience. Meditation complements prayer, in that it is time spent listening and resting in the greater silence of the soul. Taking the time to be truly still, with as serene a mind as possible, not only feels good physically but actually supports health and well-being. Meditation can lower blood pressure, enhance the immune system, and alleviate anxiety. These are benefits independent of the mystic's goal of union with God. Meditation, it seems, provides holistic benefits to every part of the soul: the body, the mind, and the spirit.

Many resources exist for the aspiring mystic to receive training in the arts of prayer and meditation. Many fine books, from traditions the world over, explore the theory and practice of cultivating a daily spiritual practice. Churches, Zen centers, open universities, and even spiritually oriented bookstores often sponsor classes or workshops on the basics of prayer and meditation. Whenever possible, it helps to receive training from a teacher or a spiritual guide. Books and classes are not just for beginners, either. The discipline of prayer and meditation requires a lifetime of learning, for the skills of the mystic way are not mere techniques that one masters, but rather the raw material of an ongoing relationship that must be lived into, day after day. Mysticism, like marriage, continually grows and evolves. Just as a married couple must give energy and attention to their relationship year after year for it to remain vibrant and healthy, so too must a mystic seek to strengthen his or her practice of prayer and meditation on an ongoing basis, in order to keep spirituality vibrant and healthy.

Therefore, no matter where we are on our spiritual journeys, we thrive when we invest time and energy to an ongoing process of learning the skills of prayer and meditation. Every aspiring mystic needs to find the path that works for him or her, and pursue it, both in study and (ideally) in working with a teacher or teachers. Study and training provides ongoing inspiration to persevere in our spiritual practice—on a daily basis, with discipline and regularity.

I have some friends who are self-employed, and in their studio they've hung a sign that reads, "Discipline is knowing what you want." It's the best definition of discipline I've ever seen. Too often we think of discipline in terms of limitation or restrictions. But the origin of the word discipline is related to knowledge passed on to a student; it doesn't have to be a negative or limiting experience at all. Discipline is being mindful of what you want, and making choices and commitments in light of that knowledge. An aspiring mystic chooses and commits to a daily practice of prayer and/or meditation.

The daily practice is one of the few things that is truly essential about being an aspiring mystic. For most of us, it is also extraordinarily difficult—but not impossible. You know the challenges we all face: work or school commitments; long, numbing commutes; family or friends with whom we want and need to spend time. Those of us involved with a church or other spiritual organization—or any organization, for that matter—find the organization itself makes a claim on our time. Then there's the daily round of housework, yardwork, paying the bills, doing the laundry . . . As hectic as life is nowadays, many people don't even get a good night's sleep. So where is the time to pray or meditate?

Here are two ways to approach this question. The first one involves rethinking our priorities. The second one involves rethinking our concept of prayer and meditation.

In rethinking our priorities, we acknowledge the many claims on our time we juggle with each day. In reviewing our busy lives, we need to consider the ways we spend time that, on inspection, seem unnecessary or perhaps not even useful. How many hours each week do we spend watching television? How many hours surfing the Internet? Playing video games? Browsing in stores? Aimlessly flipping through catalogs we've received in the mail? Reading light fiction or, for that matter, books on spirituality like this one?

A half hour a day spent in silence would equal three and a half hours each week. If you believe you are too busy to pray or meditate, please take the time to honestly evaluate your schedule. You can do it. If you can't squeeze 30 minutes a day, start with 5 or 10 minutes. But find a regular time and do it every day. Make it as non-negotiable as taking a shower or brushing your teeth.

A Flexible Understanding

Does this talk of giving up TV or the Internet sound discouraging? Many aspiring mystics lose heart when they encounter their own lack of discipline. Maybe a monk living in a remote monastery can find the time to pray or meditate for extended periods every day, but for us folks trying to balance career and family in our fast-paced world, it just doesn't seem possible.

This is often because we operate under the assumption that if we aren't praying or meditating "the right way," then we aren't doing it at all. In other words, we assume there is only one correct way to pray or meditate, and we also assume we haven't mastered that one correct way. But such thinking does little to help us along the mystic way. When we discourage ourselves for not meditating or praying the right way, we merely indulge our perfectionism and self-criticism, thereby allowing the inner voice of negativity to thwart our progress in the spirit.

It's easy to assume the "one correct way" to pray or meditate looks something like this: to wake up early in the morning, spend time reading the Bible or some other sacred text, and then kneel or sit in the lotus position, for anywhere from a half hour to an hour, the mind perfectly at rest, consciousness perfectly filled with a sense of Divine presence. If our prayer doesn't feel or look like this, we think there's something wrong. The inner critic screams, "I must be a failure."

Yes, every aspiring mystic needs to find some sort of uninterrupted quiet time when prayer and meditation is possible on a regular, disciplined basis. But we shouldn't give up if that kind of habitual practice seems elusive. Perhaps a regular practice of prayer or meditation may be thought of as a beautiful garden you are tending. If you are having difficulty planting the seeds to get the garden going, it doesn't mean you are a failure as a gardener. Probably the soil just needs some additional tilling. The soil is yourself, of course. And the additional tilling involves things you can do to cultivate a more meditative consciousness within yourself.

The keys to this additional tilling are silence, solitude, and interruption.

Everyone's life is filled with odd moments throughout the day that are either silent, or solitary, or interrupted. Reflect on how your life has moments like these: the moments when you stand in line, at the post office or the grocery store. The moments when you are the only person in the office, because traffic was light and you got to work a few minutes early. The moments when you're enjoying a quiet cup of coffee with only the morning paper to keep you company. As for interrupted moments, they include when you are on hold on the telephone, or sitting at a red light or stuck in traffic.

Each of us has many such moments over the course of the day, and paradoxically, the busier we are, the more such moments we encounter. For most people, these are the wasted times of life. But for an aspiring mystic, they are the times to do the additional tilling.

What does this "additional tilling" involve? Here's where it's important to hold a large and flexible understanding of prayer and meditation. Granted, while you are stuck in traffic or on hold on the phone, you cannot simply take a few deep breaths to enter into a deep meditative state. But you *can* choose to become more mindful of your breathing, and choose to watch your thoughts slowly come and go, and choose to be really aware of yourself and your sensations and your surroundings. You may not be able to enter into the depths of contemplative stillness, but you can recite a prayer mantra—try this: "May every moment of my day become more deeply attuned to Sacred presence." Far from being not good enough, such moments of brief prayer or semi-meditation, over time, can make a powerful difference in massaging our souls and bodies to become more supple and receptive to the Divine Presence in our lives.

It's not that the practice of prayer and meditation is an anything-goes matter. There's no substitute for a daily habit of time spent in silent devotion to the Infinite. The idea of "doing it right" haunts us because, intuitively, we recognize the value of such a stable, disciplined practice. Truly, a half hour or an hour of spiritual devotion each day is a worthy goal to strive for. But in the midst of a busy, hectic, nonstop life, we need to be gentle with ourselves. Instead of giving up because we never have time to fill the glass all the way, let's make sure we enjoy the opportunities we have to fill it part way. Prayers spoken on the run are better than no prayer at all. Scattered moments of mindfulness throughout the day are better than no meditation at all. And by allowing ourselves to pray and meditate in flexible ways, there's more hope for eventually finding the time for a deeper commitment to spirituality. The more time we give over to spiritual practice in the odd moments of our day, the more we are likely to find that the time for disciplined practice is easier to come by. And like a program of working out, a spiritual practice can build on prior success. If you can't commit to a half hour a day, commit to 5 or 10 minutes. A few minutes spent faithfully in silence each day for now can provide the foundation for 20 minutes a day next year, and a half hour a day the year after. Allow your garden to grow at its own rate—and don't stop tending it.

Time to Study

Nurturing the soul means finding ways to care for the body and the mind as well as the spirit. Prayer and meditation are the primary tools for spiritual growth and sustenance. Care of the body, as we have already noted, includes proper exercise, adequate rest, and an appropriate diet. We also need to care for our mind—and in terms of the mystic way, this means finding ways to stimulate the intellect. Spiritual seekers need to make time on a regular basis for grappling with the ideas and concepts and teachings of the great mystics of the past as well as of today.

The mere fact that you are reading this book suggests that you either enjoy, or at the very least recognize the value of, reading and study as parts of your spiritual practice. If you're like me, you might be a bookworm, someone who loves and relishes the chance to curl up with a good book. If that's you, then you probably are already doing all you need to do, and perhaps more! But many others find reading to be more of a chore than a joy. If that's you, then here are some alternatives to reading that can provide some mental stimulation:

Take a class

A teacher has many advantages over a book, including the ability to answer questions, to engage in dialogue, and to make a subject really come alive. Classes on spiritual and mystical topics can be found in most larger cities. Universities and colleges offer academic courses, while churches, synagogues, or other religious groups provide a more experiential opportunity for learning. Contact your local metaphysical bookstore; often they sponsor workshops or other learning opportunities. Taking a class not only helps you to interact with an expert in the mystical life, but it also allows you to meet and network with other spiritual seekers.

Join a discussion group

Discussion groups are similar to a class in terms of providing a social arena for your spiritual quest, but they are focused more on a topic than a teacher. Many discussion groups are organized around studying a certain book—the Bible, *A Course in Miracles, The Spiral Dance*—or a series of books all revolving around one key topic. While you will not be able to avoid the homework that either a class or a discussion group will require, you will find the conversation in such settings to be stimulating and educational in its own right.

Check out audio and video resources

Can't stand to read, but love to watch TV? You might enjoy a spiritually oriented video program. Videos from companies like Mystic Fire or Sounds True cover a variety of spiritual topics, from learning how to meditate to understanding the key themes in the world's sacred scriptures. And if you are like me, you spend far more time in your car than you'd like—but car time is great for listening to a collection of tapes, which are also available on virtually any topic of interest to the aspiring mystic—from recordings of ancient scriptures, to teaching series by popular modern-day mystics like Caroline Myss, John O'Donohue, or Thomas Keating.

Surf the Internet

Turn off the television and log onto the World Wide Web. Connect with a search engine like Yahoo and search for "mystic" or "spirituality" or "meditation" or another key word along those lines. You will find far more material than you can sensibly digest at a single sitting, or perhaps at many sittings. The only concern I would express about Web-surfing: Don't assume that it can be your entire source of mental stimulation and spiritual learning. It's very easy to do lots of skimming and browsing on the Web, and rather difficult to read more in-depth material. So use the Internet to increase your general knowledge of this (or any) subject, but don't think that cyberspace has made book-learning obsolete, for it hasn't. The Web is great for a beginner; but to master any subject still requires the resources of a library.

Stuck in Your Head

The various practices of the spiritual life—meditation, prayer, study, and reading—precisely because they are *inner* exercises, can keep us overly focused on the drama of our mental activities. After all, isn't it within the theater of the mind that mystical experiences take place, or that insights about the nature of the Sacred occur, or that moral and ethical issues are struggled with as we attempt to live a good life? In the mind. In the head. As aspiring mystics, we need to make sure we don't get stuck in our heads.

If mysticism amounts to nothing more than a head trip, several problems occur. First of all, this can lead toward neglect of the body. Who needs exercise, proper rest, and a balanced diet, when the splendors of the universe are playing out on the mental movie screen? Taken further—who needs sex or physical labor when "all that really matters" is found within? We've seen the dangers of taking this disembodied spirituality too far—such as the tragedy of the Heaven's Gate community, whose members committed mass suicide in 1997 in order to escape their physical nature and achieve transcendental purity.

Although spiritual striving may lead us to think that only the inner life matters, the facts stubbornly refuse to change. Both inner and outer, both mental and physical, both spirit and body remain essential parts of the soul. A person who is a crass materialist or a dogmatically agnostic scientist might refuse to cultivate an inner life; likewise, someone who plays the role of an "airy-fairy" mystic is just as much out of balance by living exclusively on the inner planes, having retreated from the sensual realities of the embodied world.

There's another level on which the mysticism of excessive inwardness is even more dangerous. It leads not only to neglecting our own bodies, but also to neglecting the larger body of which we all are parts—the body of the earth, and the body the entire human community. Too many spiritual seekers become so enraptured with their inner ecstasies that they cease to be concerned over questions of justice and peace and balanced living in our common life. Feeding the hungry, caring for the sick, helping women and gay and lesbian persons and people of color to secure their rightful civil liberties, calling for government and business to make solid commitments to protect the environment—these, and other tasks, are the macro equivalents of exercise and rest and good nutrition. They are the tasks we all must undertake in order to take care of our bodies, both individually and as a community.

Meditation, prayer, study, openness to spiritual ecstasies— these are the tasks of taking care of our minds and souls. But we mustn't limit our understanding of the mystical life to these inner techniques. We need to look for the presence of the Sacred in the little things we do to live well in an embodied, physical universe.

Choice and Commitment

Some traditions use the concept of magic to signify the power of spiritual growth. A magical person is someone with so much spiritual ability that wonderful things seem to effortlessly flow in his or her life. I like the concept of magic. It's gotten a bad rap, between some dogmatic religious views that regard magic as some sort of supernatural evil, and the skepticism of modern science and psychology, which sees the belief in magical powers as a form of neurosis. But I think both of these antimagical positions miss the point. The magic I believe in has nothing to do with conjuring up evil spirits or believing in the ability to suspend the laws of physics. Rather, it's magic as a practice of using will power and mind power (the imagination) to make wonderful things happen.

Consider the similarity between the words **mag**ic and **imag**ine. Both words refer to the process of weaving the mind's energies to create something new. Merely by imagining the possibility of Divine wonder flowing through my body and my spirit, I bring myself closer to manifesting my spiritual goals. But to make the dreams of the imagination come true, we need a specific kind of magic—the magic of choice and commitment, the magic of diligent action.

When I make a choice or a commitment, and I use the energies of my mind and the strength of my will to follow through on the path I've chosen, then I am using magic to make my dreams come true. Instead of having a passive relationship with life, where things just seem to happen to me, I work my magic through believing in myself and my vision—and then backing it up with the choices, commitments, and sheer effort to do what it takes to make my vision real.

For aspiring mystics, the vision involves spiritual growth and development, the cultivation of a life lived in union with the Divine. And while we cannot reduce God to a puppet, we can certainly do everything in our power to open up to the possibilities of heavenly wonder and joy.

This is what prayer, meditation, study, and the discipline of paying attention to the everyday miracles of life are all about. These are the tools we use to make the magic happen. But they are

Visualization

One of the best ways to put our hopes and aspirations into action—whether they are spiritual or "real world" hopes—is through the mental process of visualization. Briefly put, it's a process of entering into a meditative, relaxed state, and using the imaginative abilities of the mind to see that which we desire. If you desire a new job, visualize yourself hard at work in your new career environment. If you wish to lose a few pounds, visualize yourself enjoying life at your desired weight level. The process of visualization trains the mind to believe in the desired goal, thereby setting into motion the creative abilities of the mind to make the dream come true.

Visualization can play an important role in the life of the mystic. Choosing the mystical life, and committing to its disciplines, can be easier when we visualize ourselves as filled with Divine radiance, or unwavering in daily meditation, or earnest in working to help others. Those parts of the mystical life that seem difficult or hard to attain (given the frantic pace of our culture, it's amazing that anyone can meditate on a daily basis!), can more easily come within our grasp if we begin by seeing ourselves attaining—and maintaining—our desired goal.

Practical Step: Back up any choice or commitment you make for your spiritual journey with as clear a visualization of the outcome as you can muster. In your mind's eye, see yourself meditating, see yourself studying and learning, see yourself helping others. What you believe, you can achieve. Go for it!

tools—meaning they are meant to get a job done. They must be used, with diligence and effort.

In her book *Pillars of Flame*, theologian Maggie Ross asks three questions for people wishing to discern the will of the Divine in their life:

1. Where do I hurt?
2. What do I really want?
3. What price am I willing to pay?

The aspiring mystic needs to hold these questions as a guideline for the choices and commitments she makes. In many ways, the first question is an invitation to explore our woundedness, while the second question—at least for an aspiring mystic—is an invitation to honor our desire for Divine union. Now comes the third question. In order to truly open up toward the Infinite, what price *are* we willing to pay?

What price are you willing to pay for a life shimmering with the radiant presence of the Holy? What price are you willing to pay for wonder and ecstasy to be your constant companions in life? What price are you willing to pay in order to fully enter the Mysteries of life, with all the unknowing and possibility that mysticism implies?

It's the human condition to secretly hope there won't be a price to pay for something we want. I managed a college bookstore for a number of years, and I learned to feel good when my customers were complaining about the price of textbooks. I knew that if price was their *only* gripe, then I was doing a good job! In other words, no matter how low a price may be, cost-conscious consumers will want to pay even less. I recognized that college students—like everyone else—are always on the hunt for a bargain, a good deal, or a cheaper alternative. It almost seems to be part of the American Way. We say "there's no such thing as a free lunch," but we all secretly wish there were.

All this applies to the mystical life. Sooner or later, most people who feel drawn to the spiritual life are going to find that the glamour of mysticism wears off and the hard work of daily prayer and meditation is just that—a lot of work. Sooner or later, most aspiring mystics will feel it isn't fair that spirituality involves discipline, hard work, and daily commitment, especially since there is never any guarantee that we'll have a gee-whiz mystical experience. At this point, we need to remember that we're acting like a customer complaining about high prices. We want the joyous sense of Divine presence to be like falling in love for the very first time, and we want that to last throughout all our days. But mysticism is like marriage; loving God is like loving a husband or a wife. Sure, there's emotion and intimacy—and there's also dedication, commitment, and the daily diligence of doing what needs to be done.

Choose to do the work of mysticism, and then commit to it. And commit to a diligence that will see you through the unglamorous times. I'm assuming that if you've read this far in the book, you feel that the work of spirituality is a fair price to pay—or at least, a price you're willing to pay. If you don't think it's worth it to engage in daily meditation, prayer, caring for both yourself and others, and making the effort to study and learn, then you probably don't really want to lead a mystical life—at least not now. But if you are willing to pay the price, then do so. Make the commitment. Bring to it the same commitment you'd bring to a physical exercise program. A spiritual workout feels wonderful in its own way as does physically working out. Don't deny yourself that good feeling—and make it a habit.

Remember the Sabbath

All of this talk about commitment, practice, hard work, and diligence has its own danger. That danger involves the potential for workaholism. Ironically, even while we hunt for the best bargain or the lowest price, many of us harbor a lurking fear that the price we are asked to pay somehow isn't enough. We fear that we've gotten away with something, and that God won't truly bless our spiritual discipline unless we are diligent beyond compromise. Thinking we don't deserve the blessings we've received, we insist on working harder and longer than we have to. In this case, diligence becomes dysfunctional.

The Jewish tradition has the wonderful mandate to honor a sabbath day—one day a week when the community stops working for the purpose of rest and spiritual reflection. Well, to the extent that prayer and meditation are the "work" of spirituality, that means there needs to be a sabbath for aspiring mystics, too. There needs to be a regular break from the routine.

I cannot overemphasize the importance of sabbath time. Now, I'll confess that workaholism is one of my spiritual problems, and I am not always the best sabbath-keeper. But every week I have a new opportunity to do so. I am not a Jew, and so my understanding of the sabbath is not entirely traditional, but I think many people may find it useful. I see the sabbath principle as an invitation to take one day a week (Saturday, Sunday, or some other day that may be appropriate for you) and devote it to play and recreation. Seen this way, the sabbath is not a rule *against* doing something (thou shalt not work) so much as it is a positive statement *for* healthy choices (today is a day for fun and rest). Of course, the "thou shalt not" part is still important, for many workaholics like to insist that work is fun for them! And it often is. I for one genuinely like my work. But Sabbath time is meant to be an interruption, a break in the normal rhythm of life. It is a time for a different kind of fun from what we might experience the rest of the week.

This idea of interrupting work applies not only to work-as-earning-money, but also to housework and—most relevant to our discussion—spiritual practice. Again, this is a rather nontraditional approach to the sabbath, but it's something I believe aspiring mystics need. We need not only a Sabbath time away from work, but also a break from the routine of prayer and meditation and those things as well. We need a "breather," space for calm and breathing and allowing ourselves to rest. We need the space to keep our spiritual discipline from becoming spiritual drudgery.

I once took a meditation class where the teacher would have us sit in silence for anywhere from 30 to 45 minutes. Then she would ring the bell and say, "Okay, take another 10 minutes that I want to remain quiet, but you are welcome to stretch, or write in your journal, or gaze out the window—whatever." And we'd have another few minutes of silence. I always cherished those moments after the meditation, and toward the end of the class the teacher confessed to us that, for her and for many of her students, that unprogrammed time was often a time of deeper meditative awareness, precisely because we weren't *doing* anything! It was like a 10-minute long mini-sabbath rest after the work of concentrated meditation. It helped me to recognize that meditation and silent prayer, as much as they are a focus on letting go and relaxing, still remain on some level a form of work. So even this work needs to be balanced by a time of rest and play.

Work hard to maintain your spiritual commitments. Then take a breather. Take time to rest and play. Those two elements of your practice will create a rhythm with a beauty all its own.

Chapter 5

Don't Go It Alone

From the time I was a teenager through my college and graduate school years, I nurtured an ongoing interest in the spiritual life. My search for Divine presence formed a significant part of my self-identity. I eagerly read books, spent countless hours in silence and meditation, and would talk to just about anyone about the dynamics of the mystic quest. I thought spirituality and mysticism were the most important parts of my life.

But after my freshman year in college, I stopped going to church. After all, I was "spiritual but not religious."

Over the course of my university career, I became close friends with various kinds of religionists: Catholics, Lutherans, Pentecostals, Muslims, Quakers, Pagans, Buddhists, Jews—as well as people on a more secular spiritual search, often who labeled themselves as feminists, socialists, vegetarians, or peace activists. Again and again, I would patiently listen to people as they eagerly explained to me the merits of their particular path or group identity—and it always ended up sounding the same. "My way's the best way, because it's my way," is what it always seemed to be in the end. Whether a religion based its authority on the Bible, or some other book, or tradition, or nature, or a revered teacher, it always seemed to say the same thing: "We find our final authority outside of ourselves, and our job is to conform to this authority." Hmmmph! I had had enough of that with my experience growing up in the church. I was spiritual, but not religious.

While I was in graduate school I worked at the campus bookstore. Back in the textbook office, a wonderful woman named Mrs. H., old enough to be my grandmother, sat at her desk, patiently typing out purchase orders all day long (this was before the use of PCs became common). If I was working in the office, she and I would engage in conversation about this or that; she was an active member of the Episcopal Church, and so spirituality and religion would often shape our conversation.

After a while, Mrs. H. asked me why I didn't go to church. I rolled my eyes and made a semi-sarcastic comment about narrow-minded fundamentalists, to which she responded by patiently reminding me that not all churches are rigid. "Well, I don't *need* church," I said, with an impatient tone of voice that sounded more like a 15-year-old than a 25-year-old. "I'm sure you don't," she said with a generous helping of southern sweetness. "But the church needs you."

I had no witty comeback to that simple but powerful statement. In my great inner drama of rejecting religion because I thought it held me back from the spiritual free flight I so deeply desired, it never occurred to me that the point behind community was to provide opportunities to love and serve others. The words of John F. Kennedy come to mind: "Ask not what your country can do for you; ask what you can do for your country." The same principle applies to the mystical life and to the communities that invite us to share our spiritual journey with kindred souls.

Reach Out

In the last chapter, I suggested that working with a teacher or studying with a spiritual community helps us to learn prayer or meditation more effectively. I have two reasons for thinking this way. The first reason involves the inherent limitations of books or videos as teaching tools. The second reason involves the importance of other people in the mystical life.

Although books or other instructional media often contain valuable and useful information, such tools never can directly answer your personal and specific questions. If you experience difficulty with your spiritual practice, a book cannot respond to your unique situation, whereas a teacher often can. This reason alone makes it worthwhile to seek out a meditation teacher or a prayer mentor. But even more important to the mystic way is my second reason for seeking out a real, live instructor. Finding a spiritual teacher is but one aspect of mysticism not just as a spiritual practice, but as a way of life. Because the process of entering the spiritual mysteries can be so profound and life-changing, aspiring mystics shouldn't go it alone.

In saying this, I directly challenge one of the most pervasive dogmas of our culture: the dogma which holds that the individual is always more important than the group. And yes, it *is* a dogma.

In other words, it's an idea that nearly everybody believes, and because everybody believes it, everybody assumes it is as real and solid as gravity. But individualism is not like gravity. It is simply one theory about the best way to organize society.

As a society, Americans think of groups or institutions as controlling and limiting. We look to the horrors of Communism and Nazism to point out how terrible it is when people allow their lives to be managed by the "tribe." We shake our heads disapprovingly when news breaks of yet another religious cult that results in mass suicide or some other horror. Increasing numbers of Americans reject religion because the idea of conforming ourselves to the expectations of a spiritual community is too much in conflict with our belief that the individual comes first. Many of the best-selling books and most popular speakers in the field of spirituality encourage their audience to take care of themselves spiritually, and to reject any group or tribe that holds them back.

Let's inject a sense of balance into this way of thinking. For all of our commitment to individualism in our culture, most of us actually do recognize the value of community and social organization—most of the time. Few of us would accept the care of a doctor who has never studied at a medical school. We wouldn't trust a lawyer who hasn't been through the rigorous training of law school. We expect a good soldier to be obedient to his commander and loyal to his fellow troops. So why is it that we accept the idea that community and training is important to virtually every other aspect of life—but not to spirituality?

I think it relates to the problem of arrogance. Involvement with any form of community—not only spiritual community, but business organizations and other groups as well—quickly results in situations where we don't get what we want, or we are asked to do something we would rather not do. When this happens, our egoistic self thinks, "The heck with the community, I'll do it my way." And then we leave. Well, leave if you must—but remember you have just decided that your pride and autonomy mean more to you than the needs and concerns of other people. That may feel good on an adolescent level, but it's hardly in conformity with the love and compassion of the Sacred.

This isn't necessarily a plug for traditional religion or church. We can pursue mystical spirituality in communities identified with the major world religions like Christianity, Judaism, Islam, Hinduism, or Buddhism; but supportive communities can also be found in alternative or new spiritual paths like Wicca, Goddess worship, Neopaganism, or New Thought churches. Spiritual community can even arise out of study groups or workshops organized around a particular theme, book or teacher. A small group studying the writings of Francesca De Grandis or Thomas Merton could provide a wonderful and vibrant community.

If you want to be a mystic, you need a community. Exactly which form or kind of community you choose is up to you. It can be big or small, formal or informal, under the guidance of a leader or egalitarian in character. But it should meet regularly, and there should be some sense of belonging and commitment to the group. You need the support of others, the guidance of those who have gone before you, and the safety net of having someone who's willing to challenge you when you're deluding yourself.

Even the ancient Christian mystics who lived as hermits in the deserts would come together for fellowship, communal prayer, and mutual support. The point behind monasteries—historically the place where mysticism was most likely to flourish—was to provide community for spiritual seekers. You may think of the quest for the Sacred as "the flight of the alone to the alone"—but like all pilots, you need a supportive ground crew. Don't take your spiritual journey without that support.

Finding a Community

If you already have a church or some other group that supports you on your inner growth and spiritual development, congratulations! Be sure to nurture that connection, for it can prove to be one of the most important resources for your continued mystical development.

If not, you can approach finding a community as an adventure. Nearly all spiritual groups welcome visitors; finding your spiritual home should be at least as important as finding your material home. So as if you were looking for a house to buy, take your time, visit different neighborhoods, and get to know all your options. Visiting different churches, synagogues, ashrams, and other spiritual centers can be an education in itself, as well as a valuable stage on your spiritual path.

As you "shop around" for a spiritual home, keep these questions in mind: Is the community genuinely friendly? Does it seem to be the kind of place where people can hold different opinions, perhaps even disagreeing on major issues? Does it stress obedience to a master, or thinking for yourself? Is the worship ceremony interesting and beautiful? Is the group truly spiritual, or does it feel more like a social club?

Of course, many alternatives exist to traditional churches. Some of the most vibrant spiritual communities are small enough to meet in people's homes. You might even want to start such a group yourself. This is like finding an anamchara (see pages 116–117), only instead of one-on-one, a home-based spiritual community allows an entire small group of people to gather together for prayer, meditation, personal reflection, and sharing. If you do start a group, make sure it has a clear goal (like "We support each other's unique mystical development") and clear expectations over leadership and responsibilities of the members.

Practical Step: *Find, or start, a community. There's no rush; take your time to make sure the community you choose (or create) is right for you. If you're already in a community that satisfies your need for support and growth, take the time to write in your journal about why the community has been helpful. That way, if you ever need to find another community (perhaps after moving to a new city) you'll have a clear sense of what to look for.*

Balancing Freedom and Commitment

In making my plug for becoming involved with a spiritual community, I want to present a balanced view of the polarity between individual freedom and communal interaction. Balance is a key word, for a proper emphasis on our unique individuality remains important—despite how our society sometimes takes it to unhealthy extremes. America has a "my way or no way at all" mentality, which doesn't serve us well as we follow the spiritual path. Nevertheless, we also need to avoid the opposite extreme, which is the tyranny of a controlling group or community that squelches individuality in favor of the collective. We need a balance between freedom and commitment. We need community, yet we should always beware of abusive or controlling groups; we need to remember the mark of a good community is that it serves and nurtures everyone's individuality.

Community support and training are necessary in order to foster spiritual growth. But the fact of the matter is, many religious and spiritual communities fail to provide the kind of support and education that an aspiring mystic needs. Some religious groups are actually downright hostile to mysticism. They regard it as a poor emotional substitute to the robust rationality of dogma and theology. Such groups regard mysticism (and spirituality in general) as divisive and subversive. They encourage members of the group to make obedience to group leadership a higher priority than personal spiritual experience. This is obviously *not* the kind of community an aspiring mystic needs. Even if a mystic belongs to a healthy spiritual community with a balanced approach to such things as obedience and conformity, that mystic will still feel called to connect with the Divine in his or her own way. Some groups understand this, and trust that true mystical experience will, ultimately, harmonize with the group's teachings. But other groups do not always take such a generous stance toward individual spirituality.

I discovered this as a teenager. After my powerful experience of Divine presence at the Winter Celebration retreat, I soon discovered that the church my family and I belonged to—a very nice, suburban, middle-class Lutheran church—simply had no resources to deal with such intense personal experience. The pastor seemed suspicious of personal experience, at one point telling me I sounded too much like a Pentecostal "holy roller"— which he seemed to regard almost as a cult like the Moonies or the Hare Krishnas! None of the adults I knew at church seemed to have any ability to respond to my questions or experiences, either. The message was simple, and rather devastating to a teenager who didn't even ask to have a spiritual experience: "We don't do mysticism around here." Is it any wonder that I soon adopted the position of "I'm spiritual but not religious"?

Fortunately, every church or group is unique, even within the same tradition. So if one community seems hostile or indifferent to our spiritual needs, we can take responsibility for finding another context in which we can flourish and grow.

My pastor's apparent belief that Lutheranism is inherently better than Pentecostalism illustrates another common foible of even the best spiritual communities. It seems even the most liberal of groups will harbor some distrust toward ideas and teachings from outsiders. Christians will raise eyebrows when one member of their group starts to study Buddhist meditation. Southern Baptists don't really want members of their church to be devoted to the Virgin Mary. Pagans will get nervous if one of their members admits to reading the Bible. This is a normal dynamic of group membership—we keep our insiders safe by protecting them from whatever is from the outside. This kind of dynamic is not limited to religious organizations—business, government, fraternities and sororities, really all organizations have a tendency to resist anything that is foreign or alien or in any way from outside the tribe. Although this tendency plays a normal part of group dynamics, it pits the aspiring mystic into tension with the group—for most mystics intuitively recognize that spiritual truth may come at us from any direction, including from teachings and cultures outside of what our group considers "orthodox."

Every aspiring mystic needs community, but also needs to balance community involvement with an appropriate measure of trust-your-own-self individualism. Mystical seekers desire spiritual truth; and spiritual truth cuts across all religious and cultural lines. Thus, any aspiring mystic will always be somewhat at odds with the group—for the mystic will be more open to ideas and teachings that other groups members might find threatening or at least uncomfortably unfamiliar. Given this reality, spiritual seekers need to maintain community involvement for the support we can receive and the support we can give to others—but we need to acknowledge the limitations of community and be courageous when we need to pursue our spiritual path in ways that diverge from the community's modus operandi.

If you recognize that your community is not truly supportive of your mystical aspirations, it's okay to change communities. Find a new church or ashram or circle or study group. Don't make such a change lightly, or else you may be switching communities every time your ego feels slighted. Be honest in discerning whether a community is providing you the spiritual support you need. Pay attention to how much obedience the community demands of its followers, especially if such demands violate your own conscience. Use intuition and common sense to recognize the signals that it may be time to find a new spiritual home.

Many people who are spiritual individualists originally grew up in, or were otherwise involved in, a church or other religious community that didn't work for them. They left that community, but instead of looking for a healthier environment, they merely chose to reject all forms of spiritual community. Don't make that mistake—or if that's the path you've already taken, perhaps now is the time to consider finding (or creating) a truly supportive group. It's okay to leave an unsupportive community, for that clears the way to find a new and better group. It can be totally different from your old community—for example, if you leave an ultra-conservative church, you may wish to join a small, intimate (and flexible) community such as a study group for *A Course in Miracles* or a Pagan circle that meets in people's homes. What really matters with a group is how loving and supporting it is—far more than whatever the external characteristics of the group might be. Find the right group, and your mystical life will thrive.

Ask Questions

Often we resist becoming affiliated with a spiritual community or religious organization because we don't want to deal with dogma or rigid ideology. "My karma ran over my dogma" is a humorous way of saying that personal experience comes before official teachings—at least as far as spiritual matters go.

Even people who disapprove of dogma probably hold plenty of dogmatic beliefs and opinions. Dogma is not just a religious characteristic, but a defining factor of any kind of community or tribe or organization. All sorts of groups have "official" principles and teachings. Members of the National Rifle Association tend to be dogmatic about the right to bear arms. Rainbow Family folks tend to be dogmatic about governing by consensus and taking care of the environment. Scientists are dogmatic about using the scientific method to advance human knowledge. Americans as a whole tend to be dogmatic in their support of such things as individualism and the free market economy. Every group has its dogma—its beliefs and values that are shared by most or all members of the group. Dogma, in itself, is neither good nor bad—it is simply a fact of life.

Dogmat*ism*, however, is another story. Dogmatism insists on accepting something as absolutely true, even when there may be cause for reasonable doubt. Consider how some ultraconservative Christians have refused to accept the theory of evolution, even though overwhelming scientific evidence points toward its being true. Why is this? Because these ultraconservatives are dogmatic about their insistence that the Bible is the final authority on truth (and the Bible's depiction of human origins differs from evolution).

The problem with dogmatism lies not in the belief that something is true, but in the refusal to consider questions or doubts that could undermine that "truth." Dogmatism is a form of insecurity—it's a way of clinging to a belief so desperately that one becomes unable or unwilling to see evidence that calls the belief into question. This is something that everybody does. It's not just a problem that only born-again Christians or revolutionary communists suffer from. *Anyone*, no matter how conservative or liberal, no matter how naive or sophisticated, can be gripped by dogmatism.

Such inflexible thinking stunts spiritual and intellectual growth. Once we accept a dogmatic idea as true and refuse to consider possibilities to the contrary, we are in effect declaring to the universe that we don't want to grow and change anymore. The universe will happily grant us our wish—but the price we'll pay for that is spiritual stagnation.

Aspiring mystics needs to be especially concerned about dogmatism because we may encounter some extraordinary things on our journey. For example, we may experience visions and voices while meditating. If so, are they from God, or from an angel, or maybe just the product of an overactive imagination? It's tempting to think that having an extraordinary experience, like channeling a voice from another dimension, is evidence of advanced psychic ability. But perhaps it just points to a vivid imagination and the capacity for self-deception.

In my experience, having had a lovely and meaningful experience of Divine presence in the midst of a Christian communion service convinced me for some time that Christianity was the one and only pipeline to God. Several years passed by before I became disillusioned enough with the foibles of my religion to truly question my self-imposed dogma. Sure, many Christians believe their way is the only way—but there are many faithful Christians who truly do honor and respect other paths. I made the mistake of interpreting my experience according to a particular dogmatic perspective. This resulted in my coming across like a religious bigot to my high school friends—and kept me from truly appreciating the people and ideas that came to me from outside my dogmatic fortress.

The antidote to dogmatism lies in the ability to ask honest and hard questions. Aspiring mystics need the ability to be skeptical and consider alternative explanations for whatever it is we might believe or experience. Asking such questions and considering alternatives may at times seem overly cautious, but at other times it will save you from making avoidable mistakes. Most of all, the ability to ask questions and consider alternatives will keep you growing spiritually.

Question dogma. This not only makes sense for your own spiritual well-being, but it can lead to new spiritual horizons that benefit other people as well. Indeed, the great, Olympian-quality mystics often found the doorway to Divine union led through the threshold of doubt and skepticism. If powerful mystics like Jesus or the Buddha had not asked hard questions of the religious leaders of their day, they would have never been able to follow their own unique visions. If spiritual visionaries like Francis of Assisi or Martin Luther King, Jr. had not asked the questions they asked, their spiritually motivated visions of justice toward all people, regardless of wealth or race, would never have come to pass. If Goddess-worshippers like Starhawk or Carol Christ had never doubted the dogmatism that proclaimed God as only male, the spirituality of the Divine Feminine may never have come to exist like it has.

Think for yourself. Ask questions about everything. Here's a useful rule: The more something seems to be above question, the more it needs to be questioned. With every question you ask, you will eventually either find a satisfactory answer (although that answer probably will lead to even more questions), or else you will encounter the edge of mystery—which is, after all, the frontier of mysticism itself.

The Nihilist Cul-de-sac

With all this doubting, questioning, and skepticism, should we ever believe in anything?

The opposite of dogmatism, equally problematic to the mystic way, is nihilism. This is the tendency to take skepticism itself to an unhealthy extreme. A nihilist refuses to accept anything as true or to believe anything, simply hiding behind the superiority of doubt, cynicism, and skepticism. Throughout the twentieth century, nihilistic philosophy became ever more popular. "God is dead," proclaimed the leading theologians in the years following World War II, and with God's demise seemed to go all certainty, all truth, all dogma.

The spiritual term for such unrestrained doubting is agnosticism. It's very easy to say "I'm not sure if there is a God" and to use that as an excuse for not joining a spiritual community or practicing mystical techniques such as contemplative prayer or meditation. On one level, agnosticism has its place in the spiritual life—remember, question all dogma. So it's okay to ask questions about the existence of God. But that doesn't excuse us from exploring the landscape of meditation, or the dynamics of community, or the possibilities of transformative experience.

Authentic questioning can sharpen and refine our spiritual beliefs. But taken too far, nihilistic questioning can become its own dogma—the dogma of unquestioned doubt.

An agnostic who uses doubt as an excuse for rejecting even the possibility of mystical experience is someone who willingly doubts God, but refuses to question his own skepticism. Agnostic dogmatism proclaims, "only doubt and skepticism is real." But it's a spiritual dead-end: a nihilistic cul-de-sac.

We need to apply the same standards toward skepticism that we apply toward anything else. Asking questions can be a way to move into greater and more mature spiritual truth, but it can also be a way of avoiding the spiritual lessons that only come through community and practice. It's just as important to question our own motives as it is to question the dogmas of our tradition (or of any tradition, for that matter).

I mentioned earlier how as a youth I went from being dogmatic about Christianity as the only way to God, to becoming disillusioned with my religion and leaving it, at least for a time. Much of my disillusion centered about traditional Christian ideas about hell. I had been taught that God was all-loving, but also that God condemned unrepentant sinners to eternal torments. I could not reconcile how a loving God could also punish so extremely. The more people I asked about this, the more glib or pat answers I received, the more disillusioned I became. Some people even became hostile at my questioning, which only increased my discomfort. Finally, I got so fed up with the church that I rejected spiritual community altogether—that us, until I met Mrs. H. several years later.

At first, I asked a sacred question—a question about God, love, and justice. My doubt was an opportunity for me to grow in my spirituality. But when no one could help me to struggle through my doubt, I reached the point where I decided skepticism was good and dogma was bad. Years would pass before I finally began to doubt that decision—and it took that willingness to doubt my own skepticism before I could willingly reconnect with spiritual community.

So even our questioning must be questioned. If we ask questions and consider alternatives because we want to grow and mature in our spiritual lives, we are probably on the right track. But the minute our questions come from a position of self-righteousness, arrogance, or pride, then we have fallen prey to the idea that questions are better than beliefs, and only skepticism is good.

I made the statement earlier that dogma is a fact of life, and is neither good nor bad. We have a bias against dogma in our culture, because we've seen how over the ages people have held on to some pretty boneheaded dogmas ("the earth is flat," "the sun revolves around the earth," "evolution is a lie") despite all evidence to the contrary. But we do ourselves a great disservice if we decide that all dogma is therefore bad.

I personally adhere to many dogmas. I believe that God is love. I believe that daily meditation and prayer help us to increase our awareness of the presence of the Sacred. I believe that it is okay to refer to the Sacred as either God or Goddess. These are dogmas. *We all have them.* Whenever we accept a spiritual statement as true, we have accepted a dogma. This is okay, as long as we remember that no dogma is ultimately above questioning.

As you pursue the spiritual journey—through your personal daily practice, the books you read, and the people and community you interact with—remember to keep both dogma and doubt in balance. Accept the teachings that resonate with you as true, and don't be afraid to ask questions. An open and honest spirit of questioning will sometimes lead you to reject old dogmas that have outlived their usefulness, replacing them with new insights and perspectives. And eventually even those new perspectives will need to be questioned. Remember, questions sometime lead us not to answers, but to mystery. And when you encounter mystery, take off your shoes—for you are standing on holy ground.

Gurus, Spiritual Teachers, and Other Scoundrels

According to Buddhist tradition, the way to enlightenment involves taking refuge in the *Tri-Ratna*, or "three jewels": the Buddha, the Dharma, and the Sangha. The Buddha, of course, is the great world-teacher who first achieved enlightenment, and then went on to teach the Dharma—the principles and precepts by which enlightenment is attained. The Sangha is the community of people who follow this teacher and his teachings.

Each jewel within the *Tri-Ratna* requires the others in order to be effective. In other words, true Buddhist spirituality requires devotion to the Buddha, adherence to the Dharma, and involvement within the Sangha. One does not just pick and choose which of the jewels seems nice. Like three legs on a stool, they work together—or not at all.

The teacher, the wisdom, and the community: These are the three jewels of the mystical life, regardless of which path a person may follow. We've already begun to explore the deep well of mystical wisdom through the disciplines of prayer, meditation, study, and perseverance. We began this chapter by considering the importance of community. Now we need to complete the triad, and consider the role of individual teachers in the mystical life. And as important as historical figures like the Buddha or Jesus may be to the life of devotion and vision, sooner or later any serious mystic will need the guidance of a living, breathing, mentor.

A teacher, like a community, functions as the embodiment and manifestation of wisdom. Reading a book or two on the spiritual life can be valuable for whetting a person's interest, or as a reference tool to supplement the guidance of a mentor—but books or tapes, by themselves, have only limited usefulness. Mystical spirituality involves not only techniques, but subtle ways of thinking and seeing the world. For example, the technique of meditation involves more than just a proper posture—it's a way of disciplining the energy and vibration of the mind to foster the most conducive brain waves to the meditative state. Such subtle aspects of the Sacred quest must be transmitted from teacher to pupil in order to be fully grasped.

So this journey involves more than just reading a book, sitting in silence, or even joining a spiritual group. To reach our full spiritual potential, we need to take refuge in the wisdom and knowledge of our elders. We need ethical and effective teachers.

Fortunately, the great wisdom traditions have an abundance of qualified elders with wisdom to share. Virtually every medium-sized or larger city is home to several (if not literally dozens) of people who offer training, teaching, and guidance in spirituality. These "gurus" range from very traditional priests, rabbis, ministers, monks, and nuns, to the masters of non-Western religions or mystical traditions (such as Sufism, Sikhism, or Zen), to various secular or New Age trainers in the fields of meditation and consciousness expansion. Unless you live in a truly small town or rural setting, you have access to a vibrant, colorful kaleidoscope of teachers and experts who are willing to take on new students.

Some of these folks offer classes, retreats, or workshops. Others prefer to work one-on-one. Training can take place in classes that run for a specified period of time, like eight or ten weeks, or as part of a group meeting on an ongoing basis. A personal mentor can, like a therapist, meet with a student on a regular basis, or be available for

The anamchara, or soul friend

"Anyone without a soul friend is like a body without a head." So goes an old Celtic proverb about the necessity of companionship as we traverse the mystic way. The anamchara (Gaelic for "soul friend") goes back to the days of the ancient Druids, when kings and chieftains would have a Druid in their service as a personal spiritual counselor. After the British Isles became Christianized, the early Celtic saints retained the concept of the anamchara, expanding it to include any kind of friendship or committed relationship based on helping one another to grow spiritually.

The heritage of the anamchara lives on in the Christian practice of spiritual direction—the ministry of one-on-one spiritual mentoring and guidance. Other cultures have similar traditions of individuals who provide personalized mystical training: The guru of Hinduism, the shaman of many tribal cultures, and the master of Zen Buddhism all function in ways similar to a spiritual director.

But an anamchara does not have to be a spiritual master. Sometimes, the best and most helpful assistance we can receive on the mystic path will come from an ordinary friend. Truly, anyone who can walk alongside us on our spiritual journey with commitment and love can be our anamchara.

Practical Step: *Find your anamchara. He or she might be someone with extensive spiritual experience, like a minister, monk, or guru, who will provide you with mentoring. Just as likely, he or she could be another "ordinary" seeker like yourself. Commit to meeting regularly with your anamchara (once a month is ideal) for prayer, meditation, and shared reflection.*

a periodic retreat. The cost for such spiritual guidance can range from nothing, to a "love offering" (an unspecified donation), to hefty fees in the hundreds or thousands of dollars.

So how does an aspiring mystic choose his or her teacher? Of course, the smaller your particular community may be, the fewer competent teachers there will be available. But if you live in or near a major city, you will have to choose from many possible mentors. Here are some points to consider in looking for a spiritual guide:

Begin within your own tradition, but you don't have to stay there.
Working within the tradition you've grown up with—or if you
changed religions as an adult, within whatever tradition you have
chosen—makes great sense, for the symbols, stories, and rituals
of the tradition will be familiar to you. It will feel like home. This
is very useful, for the inner journey of prayer and meditation
often will lead to feelings of great emptiness, or powerful and
sometimes unsettling emotions, or a sense of being adrift or
ungrounded. A familiar and safe-feeling religious context can
help put the experiences of spiritual searching in proper perspective. So begin where you are. Sometimes, however, many
people discover that the religion of their upbringing or even of
their earlier adult conversion may not have all the resources
necessary to support a serious inner journey. So if you cannot
find a teacher within your own tradition to help you on your way,
then it is time to consider a guide from another path. To find
such a person, look to friends or loved ones for a referral—this is
far better than simply responding to an ad in the local New Age
magazine, although when all else fails, that may be the way to go.

*Be willing to pay for the training you receive—but also be sensible
about what you can afford, in both time and money.* We pay for the
services we receive from doctors, lawyers, and businesspeople;
we are willing to pay for the education we receive from college
professors or other qualified trainers. So it is only reasonable to
assume we should pay for mystical training as well. Many people
resist this idea, coming out of an old belief that a religious leader
should not sell his or her services. Some traditions do prohibit

their elders from charging set fees—but others don't, recognizing the value of fair exchange as a spiritual principle.

Like so many elements of the mystic way, balance is the key. I personally cannot support charging admission to a worship service, or charging for rituals of initiation which confer spiritual status or membership in a community (although it is good to make an offering in exchange for such spiritual services). But training and education is not the same thing as worship or ritual. Training is a service, just like any other. So be willing to pay for it. On the other hand, don't assume you must pay top dollar to get top-notch spiritual guidance. Nationally known spiritual teachers can charge in the thousands for their seminars and workshops; if you can afford such an expense, that's okay—but remember that wise guidance can also come from the local teacher whose fees are friendlier to your wallet. You can find many spiritual guides with deep wisdom to share for reasonable prices, especially associated with monasteries or other religious or nonprofit communities. Don't take on more than you can afford. And remember you are "paying" with your time as well as your money—so don't take on a class unless you have the time and energy to attend the class and to do the required work on a daily basis.

Beware of the guru who promises you the moon. Can enlightenment be had in 30 days or less? Is it possible for a weekend workshop to give you all the tools you need for rapid advancement on the mystical way? Might real salvation be possible, if only you follow the instructions of this or that spiritual guide? Some teachers will promise all sorts of wonderful results, and then dangle a hefty price tag in front of you. Run, do not walk, to the nearest exit. An important rule of thumb: Generally speaking, the more enlightened a master is, the less he or she will crow about it.

I included the word scoundrel in this section's heading partially as a joke, but also as a humorous reminder that not everyone who passes himself or herself off as a spiritual master really is one. Deciding to work with a teacher is never an excuse to abdicate our own personal power of responsibility. If your mentor proves to be more scoundrel than saint, take responsibility for finding a new mentor.

And finally, trust your intuition. This is the bottom line. Your body is usually much smarter than your brain. If something sounds good but it doesn't feel good, please trust your feelings. At the very least, be extremely cautious.

Reasonable Expectations

Look for a teacher who can instruct you in the ways of meditation and mindfulness; of nurturing discipline, commitment, and a positive attitude toward the spiritual quest. Once you find your mentor, your task is simple: to begin training, whether one-on-one or as part of a class (or both). Expect your guide to encourage you in a "can-do" attitude toward spiritual growth, but to also caution you to focus on love and service rather than on exotic spiritual experiences. A good spiritual teacher will offer you plenty of encouragement, with an occasional subtle pinprick to keep the balloon of your ego from getting overinflated. Look for that balance. If your teacher only offers big talk about spiritual fireworks, you may have unwittingly fallen for a moon-promiser.

Such a teacher may give mysticism a deliciously sexy spin, but will have little to offer when you encounter profound doubts or fears or a sense of limitation and emptiness. On the other side, some spiritual teachers take the task of deflating their students' egos to an abusive extreme. There's nothing useful in being berated or abused. If it happens to you, it's time to change teachers, immediately.

As you look for balance and perspective on the part of your teacher, be sure to keep your own expectations of the spiritual quest balanced. Do you think that working with a teacher will be the short line to ecstasy? Or perhaps you secretly hope the teacher will somehow take care of all your spiritual needs, so that all you need to do is obey the rules and follow the program? Beware of any temptation to assign too much power or control to your mentor. Remember, we cannot control or engineer the moments of ecstasy in our lives—and neither can a guru. When we choose a teacher who knows better than to promise us the moon, we need to make sure we don't secretly expect the moon anyway!

The opposite of this unrealistic expectation can be equally counterproductive—that being the tendency to believe so little in ourselves that we think even a teacher cannot help us to attain spiritual maturity. It's a mistake to think meditation and prayer or other spiritual disciplines are of no use because you don't think they'll work for you. If you don't think they'll work, they won't! But only because your belief system is holding you back. A negative attitude toward your self serves no useful purpose whatsoever.

Fortunately, we can be as liberated by positive beliefs as easily as we can be held back by negative ones. Believing in the possibility of mystical experience, or the usefulness of prayer, or the magic that a mentor can work in your life, all can have profound and wondrous effects on the shape of your spiritual journey. You never know—the Great Mystery could just decide to make you the next great mystic, filled with unlimited, pulsating ecstasies of indescribable splendor. It *is* possible! And even if you never attain that Olympian level of Divine union, the more you believe in possibilities, the more wonder you *will* experience. So don't limit yourself. Bear in mind that a good mentor will stretch your abilities beyond what you previously thought possible.

Chapter 6 # The Landscape of Letting Go

One of my more memorable spiritual adventures involved my first encounter with a Lakota sweatlodge. It was the spring of 1991. The previous winter, I became swept along with the widespread rush of enthusiasm for Native American culture that followed the success of Kevin Costner's *Dances With Wolves*. Being a pureblooded Euro-American from the East Coast, I had almost no knowledge of Indian spirituality and religion, but I was interested in the Goddess revival and earth-centered spirituality, and Native American beliefs and practices struck me as being somewhat similar in terms of its nature orientation. About this time I attended a lecture by a Native writer named Ed McGaa, Eagle Man. At the reception I met a woman from Alabama who owned a small nature preserve where she and her half-Lakota husband practiced the Red path. To my white delight, she invited me to come participate in a sweatlodge.

For my readers who may not be familiar with a sweatlodge, it is basically a small dome-shaped structure in which an intense purification ritual takes place. After being heated in a bonfire, rocks are placed in a pit in the middle of the lodge; the sweatlodge leader pours water over the heated rocks, with tons of steam being the obvious result. Thus, participants endure heat and steam in a small, dark chamber, praying and chanting all the while. This process not only purifies the body (thanks to the sweat that washes toxins out of the system), but provides a spiritual cleansing as well, both through the ritual and prayers, as well as through the experience of enduring the intensity of the experience.

When the day arrived for my sweatlodge experience, I drove to Alabama and helped build the temporary lodge and collect wood for the fire. Finally about a dozen people entered the lodge, crawling into the small chamber (only about four feet high at its highest point) and filling the tiny space with our already-perspiring bodies. Soon the lodge leader crawled in, calling to the firetender to bring in the rocks, or "Grandfathers" as he called them. While the heated rocks were brought in, one at a time, held by a pitchfork, the leader explained that we would experience four rounds of sweat, with chanting and prayers during each round. "It gets hot in here, *really* hot," he warned us. "There's no shame in realizing you've had enough. Just call out *'mitukaye owasin* (Lakota for all my relations), open the door,' and we'll let you out." I listened disinterestedly. There was no way I was going to leave the sweatlodge before the ritual was over; I was there to experience it to the fullest.

Finally the last of the rocks were brought in and laid in the small pit in the center, surrounded by all of our knees as we sat cross-legged or kneeling in a circle. The rocks glowed and sparkled, and smelled of the fire. After the last rock, the door to the lodge was shut, and we were in utter darkness, broken only by the soft glowing of the rocks.

Hisssss went the water as the first cupful was poured over the rocks. Clouds of steam rose up, assaulting us. My face tingled with an unpleasant warmth, and I closed my eyes. More hissing, more steam. The heat increased. *This is nothing*, I thought. *Not even like a sauna.*

Then came another blast of steam, and another, as the leader kept pouring the water. Suddenly I realized this was no second-rate sauna. I thought my pores were going to pop, they were pumping out so much sweat. Even breathing became a chore, the heat seeming to singe my lungs from the inside out.

Oh, God, I thought with an inner moan. I was about to die.

Instinctively I bent over, straining to get my face as close to the cool earth as possible. As a wave of steam seemed to roll like fire ants across my back, my mouth and nostrils gasped for joy and survival as I gulped in the cool air at ground level. My cheek sank with utter relief into the muddy earth, and I lay there, utterly amazed that my heart continued to beat.

So much for this being nothing.

Finally the leader stopped pouring water and started to drum and chant. Sweat pouring out of me like a river raging through a broken dam, I focused on the prayer as best I could. Finally, the leader called for the door of the lodge to be opened—so fresh new hot rocks could be brought in. The first round was over. Only three to go!

I did make it through the entire ceremony. But in the process, I had to give up my bravado as well as my rather patronizing approach to "experiencing an Indian ceremony." I crawled into the lodge with the smug grin of someone who collects religious experiences like boy scout merit badges. An hour later, I crawled out with a newfound respect for the power of the elements and a humble sense of gratitude for my body's ability to endure.

When I jumped into the cold stream near the lodge to wash off the last sheen of perspiration and dirt from my body, I felt as if I had been truly reborn.

Attachments

The mystic journey is a path of letting go. This is true when it involves a letting go such as I experienced in my sweatlodge—letting go of my smug feelings of bravado and my rather proud self-image of being invulnerable to the steam's power—but on a more fundamental level, mystical letting go means detaching ourselves from anything unreal, illusory, or inimical to our spiritual growth. From addictions to the human capacity for violence, the spiritual seeker has much to surrender as he or she progresses along the mystic way.

Great mystics work hard to cultivate a sense of detachment in their lives—detachment not only from material things, but from mental or spiritual qualities (like arrogance or nihilism) as well. Although my sweatlodge experience taught me that sometimes letting go can be thrust upon us, a mystic seeks to be proactive in the process of detachment. The first step toward this proactive spiritual detachment involves acknowledging the *attachments* that are at work in our lives.

It's a common misconception that mysticism involves extremely rigorous and almost vicious self-denial. A mystic is seen as an austere, ascetical monk who denies himself all creature comforts (especially sex), fasts regularly, prefers to wear horsehair shirts, and flogs himself daily in order to "mortify the flesh." Who in their right mind would want to pursue such a life-denying spirituality?

Fortunately, the masochistic monk is little more than a caricature—most mystics, both in the past and certainly in the present, would disavow such self-punishment, for reasons I will explain shortly. But unfortunately, it is a persistent stereotype that serious spirituality, at least in a religious context, involves obsessive self-denial. Unless we are willing to take on such an austere challenge, we have no business pursuing the mystical way.

But this misconception misses the point of true letting go.

The great mystics of old wrote repeatedly about the necessity of ridding ourselves of attachments. The problem, according to the mystic masters, was not in pleasure and creature comforts themselves—it is the *attachment* to such pleasures and comforts that creates an obstacle to the spiritual life.

What is an "attachment"? Probably the closest modern word to mean the same thing would be addiction. But even that doesn't come close enough, for we tend to think of an addiction as involving something which, if given up, would cause us to go into physical withdrawal. We know that nicotine, alcohol, and narcotics are addictive, for when an addict stops using one of these substances, he or she will experience wrenching and sometimes even life-threatening physical discomfort as the body adjusts. An attachment is like an addiction, only it functions on a spiritual level—meaning that giving up an attachment may not cause physical withdrawal, but it may well cause a sense of spiritual pain and discomfort that is in its own way a "withdrawal."

Any behavior that diminishes our freedom usually involves an attachment. If I say I want to be an artist, but never seem to find the time to paint because I'm so busy watching TV, then I've got an attachment to the tube that is keeping me from living my dreams. Or if I want to lose weight but never manage to do so because I can't bear to go without my daily candy bar in the afternoon and dish of ice cream at night . . . you get the point. We can be attached to almost any thing that provides us some sort of pleasure while at the same time denying us the freedom to do something else we want to do. The three most powerful kinds of

Letting Go of Attachments and Addictions

In the recovery system of Alcoholics Anonymous and other 12-step programs, Step 1 involves admitting to ourselves when we have a problem. This is true whether it is a life-or-death addiction like alcoholism, or even a relatively mild attachment like the tendency to watch too much TV. Chances are, every one of us has some attachments that we could let go of—but first, we have to admit they're there.

Your journal can be an important tool in this process. Reviewing what you've written over several months or years, patterns will *emerge. Things we complain about over and over again, without ever seeking to solve the problem, can indicate an attachment. Equally important are the things that are conspicuous in their absence. If I'm 50 pounds overweight, I might never "bother" to write about food in my journal. Examine yourself for your self-inflicted blind spots.*

Once we identify our attachments, how do we let go of them? If it's as serious as alcoholism or an eating disorder, professional help (or the very least, a 12-step group) may be necessary. Even with our lesser attachments, we often need the support (and accountability) of a therapist or an anamchara before we can shake off the bad habit. If you resolve to shed something that's holding you back, don't keep it to yourself! Your friend will be proud of you for making the effort to grow, and will be there for help when temptation comes for a visit.

Practical Step: *Write down your attachments and addictions. Visualize how much more powerful your life will be without them. If it's a serious problem, get professional help. Even with less serious attachments, share your resolve to grow with a trusted friend—and do it.*

attachment involve money, sex, and power. This is why monasteries have traditionally asked their new members to take vows of poverty, chastity, and obedience. It's not that there's anything particularly holy about obedience or celibacy or poverty. But the focus on these vows allowed a monk to dodge the bullet of potential attachments that could prevent his growth in the Spirit. Of course, most aspiring mystics today have families and careers instead of monastic vocations; so we must learn how to forgo attachments to money, sex, and power without merely renouncing them.

Why are attachments problematic? The traditional language of mysticism states that attachments separate us from God. A more modern approach would see attachments as separating us from our own freedom and our own highest desires—therefore, they separate us from our very selves. And really, separation from our own highest good and separation from God amounts to just about the same thing. For example, if it's more loving to lose weight than to eat candy bars, but I insist on eating the chocolate, I am denying myself love. I suppose I'm loving myself a little— after all, candy tastes good—but it's a limited love, since getting fit would be the greater and more loving choice. In denying myself love, does it matter whether that love is coming from God or from my higher self? Either way, it is my attachment (in this case, to candy) that stands in the way of my greatest freedom and love.

Unfortunately, the only way to give up attachments is to give up the attachment. Which means, whether you're attached to watching TV, or shopping, or drinking, or surfing the Internet, or whatever—the only way to let go of that attachment is to modify your behavior. With some attachments and addictions (like alcohol or nicotine), that usually means stopping the compulsive behavior altogether. Other attachments, such as to eating or to working, cannot be given up totally, but must be altered in a way that is healthy and life-enhancing. Either way, the pain of spiritual withdrawal will ensue. This is one reason why having spiritual friends and/or a spiritual community is essential to the mystical life. Aspiring mystics need support when they let go of an attachment.

Mystics of old sometimes had a reputation for self-inflicted floggings and wearing horsehair shirts. They used such austere practices as strategies for giving up their attachments. I cannot speak as to how successful such practices are for spiritual seekers (frankly, they sound rather kinky to me!). But in modern times most mystics disavow such extreme self-punishments, for two reasons.

First, it is wrong to think we must hate or abuse ourselves in order for God to love us. That is an absurd, grotesque misconception of what mysticism is really about. I personally have no interest in worshipping a deity who wants me to hate myself. On the other hand, a God who wants me to love myself enough to grow and mature is a God worthy of my devotion.

The second reason why self-denial can be a trap is that *it can be an attachment in itself.* Have you ever met a vegetarian who insists on putting down anyone who eats meat? Or a former alcoholic who cannot stop criticizing anyone who drinks, even those who drink responsibly? These people are as attached to their austerities as others are attached to their indulgences.

There's an old Buddhist story about two monks walking through the woods. They reach a stream, where a beautiful woman is standing. She doesn't know how to swim and cannot cross the water. So one of the monks offers to carry her across. She accepts, and crosses the river in his arms. She thanks the monk, and he and his companion continue on their way. Several miles later, the other monk finally blurts out, "I cannot believe that you, a monk with a vow of chastity, could have actually carried that woman across the stream like you did!" The first monk replies,

"You know, I left the woman back there by the riverbank, but it appears that you are still carrying her."

The message is simple: Our efforts for self-discipline can become attachments as easily and surely as can our acts of indulgence. These "inverse attachments" can cripple our spiritual maturity just as surely as any other behavior that limits our freedom. How do these inverse attachments limit our freedom? In the most insidious way of all—they limit us from being truly humble.

Notice your attachments. Notice the things you do that you think you shouldn't, or the things you do that keep you from reaching a higher goal. Noticing your attachments is the first step toward letting go of them. But beware replacing an attachment with an inverse attachment. Replacing materialism with spiritual pride will not further you on the road to mystical freedom.

Living with Attachments

If you are like me, and I suspect like most people, the disciplines of mysticism will sooner or later make you aware of just how many attachments, big or small, you actually have. For example, consider my attachments: I am attached to writing, to reading, to working, to surfing the Internet, to sweets and fatty foods, to collecting books, to music (all the way from Vaughan Williams to Grateful Dead), to *Star Trek*, to religion and spirituality, and I'm sure there are others I'm not thinking of right at the moment. Yes, even religion and spirituality can be an attachment. To a greater or lesser extent, my attachments are preventing me from exercising, from gardening, from political activism, and even from being a better housekeeper.

Of course, not all of my attachments are as problematic as the others, and fortunately, none of my attachments are as life-threatening as alcoholism or cigarette addiction (although as I age, I'm beginning to realize the jig is up with the fatty-food addiction!). But there they all are, and I recognize that I couldn't give up any of them without experiencing some measure of psychic or spiritual distress. In short, I have many attachments—as do we all.

Aspiring mystics can quickly fall into the trap of trying to root out all of our attachments, with vigor and vigilance—quickly making ourselves (and probably everyone around us) miserable in the process. Such zeal marks the first step toward the inverse attachment to self-denial and austere asceticism.

Psychologist Gerald May suggests in his book *Addiction and Grace* that addictions are little more than attempts to control or master life. That's obvious with addictions like drugs or alcohol, for those substances are used to control feelings. But even the little attachments, like indiscriminate credit card spending or compulsive exercising, often represent attempts to manage our feelings or to feel safe and in control of a chaotic and unpredictable world. The truth, however, is that we are *not* in control. We will eventually die; we may suffer considerably before our death; even worse, we will stand by helplessly as those we love suffer and die. We feel our own powerlessness when faced with the injustices and atrocities of the world. We are not in control. We forge addictions and attachments as ways of trying to forget our lack of control. So even when we attempt to master our attachments by rooting them all out, we soon discover that is nothing more than another attempt to manage and control.

I'm not suggesting there's no point in trying to let go of attachments. The mystical journey is a quest for deeper love and freedom, and therefore part of the way we make ourselves worthy to receive the presence of the Great Mystery is by striving to improve ourselves. But this must be balanced by humility. Ultimately, we cannot make ourselves perfect, although we all wish we could. And what is perfection, after all? Maybe when the day is done we will discover that, in the eyes of the Creator, we are already perfect.

Notice all your attachments, but only work on letting go of one or at the most two at a time. As I write this, I'm working on letting go of the fatty foods. I'll worry about how I spend too many hours surfing the Internet later. Instead of pouring all your energy into rooting out your attachments, put a little bit of energy into gradual self-improvement—and save the rest of your energy for learning simply to love and accept. Love and accept yourself, love and accept others, and love and accept God. The part of ourselves that wants attachments is the part that doesn't understand how love is better than control. The best way to heal that part is not by taking something away, but by creating something new: genuine, accepting love.

Sacrifice

Related to the concept of letting go is the concept of sacrifice. Mahatma Gandhi once made a list of "Seven Blunders"—problems that he saw as the root of violence, inequality, and other social ills. The list included such blunders as "pleasure without conscience," "science without humanity," and "commerce without morality." But probably the most startling blunder on Gandhi's list was "worship without sacrifice." Gandhi knew, as did many mystics and saints before him, that the spiritual life must include an element of sacrifice. Mysticism without sacrifice is like a body without a soul.

Sacrifice is one of the most misunderstood parts of spirituality. To many people, the word means nothing more than a painful loss—an outgrowth, perhaps, of the idea that someone who dies for his country has made "the ultimate sacrifice." If we sell our car at a value far below its blue book listing, we are making a sacrifice. If we cancel a vacation because our office is understaffed, it's another sacrifice. No wonder the idea of sacrifice seems distasteful, for who likes the idea of pain and loss? The religious dimension of sacrifice conjures images of primitive rituals involving human or animal sacrifice—the taking of an innocent life in order to appease a terrible deity. That's enough to give most civilized people a shudder. Sacrifice? No thanks.

Yet Gandhi's warning against a worship without sacrifice demands our attention. Gandhi knew that the true spiritual value of sacrifice lies in something far different than mere loss or the horror of ritual killing. Indeed, the true meaning of sacrifice has been lost over the last few centuries as our society has become more and more secularized and technological. Originally from the Latin *sacer facere*, a sacrifice meant simply the performance of sacred rites. But what kind of sacred rites call for a sacrifice, and how did this spiritually neutral word come to have such a connotation of loss?

To answer this question, we need to consider the role and importance of exchanging gifts. When two people fall in love, isn't it normal for part of the courtship ritual to involve the exchange of gifts? We think of a suitor showing up at the door of his beloved's home, carrying chocolates and flowers. Marriage ceremonies often involve the exchanging of gifts—the rings that the bride and groom offer to one another as tokens of their love. And gift-giving is not just limited to our romantic partners, either. Birthdays and the December holidays are times when we offer gifts to not just husbands and wives, but other family members and close friends as well.

Part of the way we show our love for another is by the offering of gifts. We have strong beliefs about the rules behind such gift-giving—for example, "it's not the size of the gift, but the thought that counts," and "it's better to give than to receive"—rules which, by their very existence, show how important such gift-giving is. "It's better to give than to receive" reminds us that the way to be loved is by first loving others; "It's the thought that counts" reminds us that even a humble and seemingly unworthy gift is a necessary and important part of the ritual of love.

What works on the human-to-human realm also works on the human-to-divine realm. Part of the mystery of life is the inexplicable fact that we exist at all; it is a mystery to live, to have the ability to experience pleasure and pain and to make choices in order to maximize the pleasure. None of us created this for ourselves—our very lives are gifts we have received, from the source of the Great Mystery, by way of our parents.

When we think about it, everything we have, even the things we've earned, are gifts we have received from the universe. It is the marvelous world we live in that provides the food we eat, the resources necessary to create art and technology, the majestic mountains and beaches where we find relaxation and recreation. Everything we have is, on some level, a gift. And all of these gifts come from the Great Mystery, the Goddess, the Universe, God.

So in the majestic love affair of the spiritual life—the love affair between you and the creator of all things—what gifts do you offer? What tokens of your love can you bring to the presence of the mystery, and lay down as an offering to the Sacred?

Here is where we find the original meaning of sacrifice—the meaning that Gandhi saw as important. In ancient times many spiritual traditions included the offering of animal or even human sacrifice—where a life was given to the gods. Of course, it is now unthinkable to offer a life as a sacrifice, but this does not mean we no longer need to offer gifts to the Sacred. Over time, primitive forms of sacrifice were replaced with the practice of offering money, or time and energy to the Sacred. Today, religious organizations from the Episcopalians to the Druid revivalists talk about making sacrifices of prayer, praise, and thanksgiving.

As you make your way on the mystical journey, ask yourself what kind of gifts you wish to offer to your loved one—God, the Great Mystery, the Source of all ecstasy and meaning and joy. Each of us, no matter how modest our earthly possessions may be, has much to offer in terms of time and talent, as well as treasure. Reflect on what you have to offer to the Great Mystery. Remember that, in order to make your gift a true sacrifice, it needs to be offered in some sort of ritual or ceremonial way. Your spiritual community or soul friend can help you to find or to write a ritual that will work for your gift. You may perform your ceremonial sacrifice privately, or with others. It does not have to be elaborate, by any means—it's just important that you intentionally say to the gods, "Here I am, and I am making this offering to you, as a way of saying I love you and as a way of saying thank you for all you have given me."

Masochism: No Thanks

True spiritual sacrifice does not necessarily have to involve pain and loss. It can be a joyous thing, just as giving a gift to someone we love can be joyous, no matter how expensive the gift may be. In fact, when a sacrifice feels heavy or burdensome or full of pain and loss, we should at the very least ask ourselves what's going on, why is this gift costing so much as to rob the experience of joy? Perhaps we have a hidden or unconscious motive we need to be aware of, a part of ourselves that needs healing. If I give something to the Sacred only out of a sense of duty or obligation, my sacrifice will undoubtedly feel painful. Even worse, such painful emotions could create an internal block between me and the Divine—meaning I am denying myself the flow of love between me and God.

For sacrifice to be joyful does not mean that the gift is necessarily only a little gift. Joyful is not the same thing as easy. Sometimes the best sacrifices are the ones that stretch us—not to the breaking point, but to the point of realizing that we have more to give than we had previously thought. This connects with letting go of attachments. One of the best sacrifices we can make is to give our attachments to the Sacred. What we are really giving is a commitment to maturity and freedom, but on a ritual level it makes the most sense to ceremonially sacrifice the attachment itself. "God, I give to you my tendency to watch too much TV"; "Holy One, I sacrifice my overeating habits to you"; and so forth. These sacrifices are joyful, but are by no means painless! Here, keeping sacrifice on track is a matter of perspective. The pain of surrendering the attachment is, at least in the long run, overshadowed by the joy of cultivating greater freedom and power in one's life and spirituality. Perhaps this is the best way to make sense of sacrifice's grim reputation. Yes, it is possible to make a painful sacrifice. But as long as the pain of the sacrifice is small compared to the pleasure of offering gifts to the Spirit of Love, then it can be a truly joyful sacrifice.

Sacrifice should be big enough to matter, but not so big as to be masochistic. Remember the poor medieval monk with his flog and his horsehair shirt. Mortifying the flesh seemed like a good idea at the time, but today we recognize it as a form of self-hatred, doing little to glorify God and a lot to cause needless pain and suffering. Whatever gifts you offer to the Sacred, take care that they are not your "horsehair shirt." Whatever pain or loss your sacrifice entails must clearly serve a higher purpose of love and freedom.

Harm None

Christianity teaches, "If someone strikes you on one cheek, turn and offer him the other."

Judaism teaches, "You shall not kill."

Wicca teaches, "Do what you want, as long as you harm no one."

In Buddhism, the first *shila* (obligation or precept) for followers of the dharma is the call to nonharm.

Nonharm or nonviolence are central spiritual principles the world over. Thanks to the reality of dangerous inner cities, random shootings on our highways, in our schools, and in our shopping centers, not to mention the threat of terrorism or the bloodshed of regional wars—this religious call to nonharm seems almost like an unattainable ideal. But this is a fundamental precept of spirituality, universally present in the teachings of enlightened masters everywhere. It is something that every aspiring mystic must grapple with. Part of the territory of cultivating a relationship with the Holy One includes letting go of your own tendency to violence, no matter how small or large it may be.

The impulse to violence knows no boundaries. It may appear in men or women, rich or poor, young or old, educated or ignorant. It is a universal problem. And it doesn't always manifest in terms of sheer aggression. Bloodthirst can masquerade as self-righteousness, often directed at criminals ("The electric chair is too good for the likes of him!") or war enemies ("That dictator needs to be drawn and quartered."). It can be motivated by fear and rage, but can also come out of such noble aspirations as the desire for self-protection or a sense of fairness and justice. But no matter what its origin or how pure (or impure) its motivation, the impulse to harm is an attachment to hatred—whether that involves a sanitized death row execution by lethal injection or the horrific terror of a drunk husband beating his wife.

Why do we so easily succumb to the desire to harm others?

The impulse to violence derives from inability to manage anger and a dysfunctional need to control others. We harm others because we think doing so will meet our needs. But mystical wisdom insists this is an illusion. Or, we harm others because we simply have not learned to behave in appropriate ways as a result of anger or rage. It's important to note that the commandment to refrain from harming others is not a commandment to stuff our feelings. Anger and rage are natural, human responses to situations that seem threatening, dangerous, or frustrating. The problem of harm is the problem of using such strong feelings as fuel for punishing or controlling others, rather than as fuel for taking responsibility for making things better.

The temptation to harm others does not just play out in terms of "real" violence, involving guns and blood. We can harm in many ways, most of which do not involve physical death. We can abuse and neglect others. We can ignore the suffering of others, deciding that our own comfort is more important than easing the pain of another. We can make it a habit to belittle others, from our children to our political or business rivals, ensuring that our own sense of control and power is never threatened by the concerns or needs of someone else. In scenarios like these, we cause harm, no matter how slight. We have chosen self-protection over being in relationship. And whether the fruit of that self-protection is simply ignoring others or actively abusing them, some level of spiritual, mental, or physical harm results.

The call to nonharm may seem like an overwhelming challenge. "I can make sure I never kill anyone, but how can I prevent myself from being neglectful or ignoring the needs of others? I can barely walk down the street without confronting the needs of a dozen homeless persons!" True enough. Any aspiring mystic quickly learns that he or she cannot alleviate the sufferings of the world, even though he or she will probably always try (and when tempered by humility, such efforts to help alleviate the sufferings of others, even on a limited scale, are filled with Divine light). But every mystic can, and should, make it a practice at the very least to

Being Peace

Thich Nhat Hanh, a Vietnamese monk and respected author, developed the concept of "being peace" as a way of living mindfully and meditatively in the midst of life's busy pace. Being peace is not just for monks, nuns, and saints. It is a concept that anyone can incorporate into her or his daily life.

To be peace means honoring peace not as something we have to create or make but rather simply allowing it to be who we are. Peacefulness resides in the simple act of breathing in and out, of resting in the present moment, and in learning to allow life to flow, rather than trying to control everything. Being peace means taking the mystical disciplines of meditation and contemplation with us as we foray into the world, remaining mindful of deep breathing and relaxed awareness as much as possible every moment, moment after moment, throughout the day.

It's not easy, of course. It requires a constant habit of letting go, an ability to return to centered breathing and peaceful awareness of the present moment, again and again, throughout the course of every

busy and distracting day. But efforts made toward being peace can reward us richly, with a subtle sense of well-being and of carrying the Divine presence with us, everywhere we go, every moment of the day.

Practical Step: *Begin your day with a resolve to practice peace. An affirmation like "Today I will carry the principles of meditation and being peace with me throughout my day" can help. As you repeat the affirmation, visualize yourself calm and breathing deeply at various moments of the day. As your day progresses, allow yourself moments of recentering whenever the thought of meditation or peace crosses your mind. Of course, be careful not to become too relaxed while driving!*

refrain from adding to the sufferings of the world—and this is done by refraining from harming others.

But this isn't just about what you "can't do." Refraining from harming or abusing others needs to be coupled with an active effort to nurture compassion and goodwill toward others in your life. Otherwise, it's like going on a diet without making any effort to establish good eating habits—a practice that usually results in only a temporary weight loss, before the old habits come roaring back, seemingly stronger than before. So the effort to curb unloving behavior needs to be balanced by an equally strong effort to develop loving ways of relating to others—whether the "other" is a family member or friend with whom you regularly experience conflict, or a business rival, or even just a person on the street who needs a bite to eat.

Complete the Circle

One of the dangers of taking on the task of not harming others, or practicing compassion to others, is the temptation to neglect our own needs in our efforts to protect or help others. If, in order to keep from lashing out at someone, I turn all my anger inward and slowly give myself an ulcer or cancer in the process, I may have refrained from harming others but not without harming myself. Or, if in order to help alleviate the suffering of others, I refuse to allow myself any rest or luxury, I have undermined my own efforts of spiritual love.

The call to nonharm is not just about other people. We have to treat ourselves—our very own body, mind, and soul—with the same respect and compassion and goodwill that we offer to anyone else. For many people, including many spiritual seekers, this is the hardest task of all. It's so easy to neglect the self, thinking that such behavior is a strategy for spiritual advancement ("I need to purify my ego in order to be worthy of Divine love"), when all it really does is inflict a nonsustainable burden on yourself.

The Golden Rule applies here. "Treat others the way you would have them treat you" can be paraphrased like this: "Treat yourself with the same compassion you show to others" or "Treat yourself the way you think others should treat themselves." In doing so, you complete the circle, and your entire being becomes dedicated to serving love and compassion—for *all* beings, not just the ones outside of your skin.

Ironically, harming others—or even wanting others to be harmed—is a way of harming ourselves. Why? Because the rage and fear that forms the raw emotional foundation of harm erodes our capacities for love, forgiveness, mercy, and compassion. When we are attached to the energies of harm, we have created a block between ourselves and the energies of Divine love. We cut ourselves off from the lifeblood of the universe because of our attachment to making (or seeing) someone else suffer.

The call to nonharm is the highest call of surrendering attachments. When we let go of the impulse to control others, we become truly free to love. This is not simple, of course. Given the violence in our world, many of us want to protect ourselves and our loved ones. We want to carry concealed weapons, so if some crazy lunatic ever walks into our office with a rifle and opens fire, we can fight back. Or we want the death penalty because we want the toughest possible deterrent. Unfortunately, the mystical life never promises us that if we only commit to nonviolence and nonharm, God will magically protect us from the violence of others. Alas, it doesn't work that way. The impulse to self-protection symbolized by such things as concealed weapons and the death penalty is certainly understandable, but it is simply not the way of the mystic. In an escalating situation of imminent violence, somebody has to be the first to take his or her finger off the trigger or else tragedy will certainly result. We who believe in the love and ecstasy of God have the responsibility of being the first to say "no more violence."

Choosing the path of nonharm is not the same as being a doormat or a wimp. After all, Gandhi (the foremost advocate of nonharm in recent history) successfully led a peaceful uprising that contributed to his country's independence. Martin Luther

King, Jr. helped to bring about social change in American race relations, using radical but nonviolent tactics. If such visionaries could successfully contribute to social change without resorting to violence, then certainly aspiring mystics like you and me can learn to live according to principles of nonharm and compassion toward others in our daily lives, whether that means being more compassionate toward family members, business rivals, political opponents, or even people who frighten us (such as criminals or those of ethnic or economic backgrounds different from our own). Love and harm cannot coexist. Letting go of the impulse to harm means creating space within your soul for love.

Chapter 7 # Relating to the Mystery

To understand the way of the mystic, we need to think in terms of relationship. A mystic does not merely think about God, or "believe in" God, or worship the Divine. To be a mystic means *to love*—that is, have a relationship with—the Divine Mystery. Just as we relate to our spouse, our parents, our children, our friends, and our business associates, so too do we find mystical spirituality is an ongoing process of love and intimacy—a relationship.

Relationships are complex matters. They involve agreements and understandings (or, all too often, misunderstandings). They can be helped or hindered by the assumptions and unspoken expectations held by each party in the relationship. They thrive best in an environment of communication—which means not only speaking, but listening.

As we progress along the mystical way, more and more we'll see how the dynamics of relationship apply to spirituality—just as surely as they apply to all our human relationships.

Imagine a man and a woman who get married. The man has a naturally jealous temperament, while the woman is open and trusting. The man assumes that his wife might at any time be unfaithful to him—he thinks that the minute she meets someone who is in the least bit attractive to her, she'll hop into bed with him. Now the woman, on the other hand, assumes that, since both she and her husband made a promise to each other, they will honor that promise. Only something truly extraordinary could lead to either of them having an affair.

So not long after they get married these two go to a party at a beautiful house full of attractive, well-dressed, successful people. Everyone is mingling and enjoying themselves, and before long the man is having a delightful conversation with a beautiful woman. But in the middle of their conversation, he sees his wife moving toward them, so he abruptly breaks off speaking with the beautiful woman and makes a beeline to the bar, where he gets another drink.

Now he looks for his wife, and he is appalled to see her laughing and smiling as she talks to the host of the party—a prominent lawyer and extremely eligible bachelor. Flushed and angry, he goes directly to her and whispers in her ear that he's developed a sudden headache and they must leave immediately.

On their way home, they have a huge fight over something entirely irrelevant.

So what's going on here? Our newlyweds suffer from a clash of hidden assumptions. The husband assumes that people tend to be unfaithful and unreliable. He may have been wounded as a child, or may be harboring guilty feelings from a time when he was unfaithful to someone he loved. Whatever the reason, he now has an assumption that colors the way he sees his wife—and even the way he thinks she regards him. After all, he was just as embarrassed when she saw him talking to another woman as he was angry at her talking to another man. Meanwhile, the wife assumes people are basically trustworthy, and therefore thought nothing of her husband enjoying the conversation with another woman—or, for that matter, thought nothing of her own conversation with the host.

Our relationships are shaped, influenced, and colored by our assumptions and beliefs regarding human nature and behavior, power, morality, and various other issues, both practical and philosophical. What we believe and assume about life shapes who we are and how we interact with others. Sometimes our assumptions are hidden—even hidden from ourselves. Just as the husband at the party barely recognized how his assumption caused his jealousy, often our experience is shaped by ideas and beliefs that lurk below our conscious mind—but that can wreak havoc on how we experience life.

This power of assumptions affects more than just our human-to-human relationships. Our relationship with the Sacred also reflects our assumptions—not only about life and love, but also about the great Mysteries that we encounter on the mystical frontier. As we progress on the journey of seeking closer union with the Divine, we must acknowledge our assumptions and learn to recognize our hidden beliefs, or else they could secretly hold us back from the ecstasy we desire.

In terms of spirituality, these hidden assumptions could include beliefs you hold about God, beliefs you hold about yourself, or beliefs you hold about mysticism. Let's look at these one at a time. Do you think God is angry, or wrathful? Do you think God will punish you or somehow get back at you when you do something that displeases him? Or, do you think the Sacred is really so vast and huge that there's no way God could even care about you? Do you think God is unreliable, or worse yet, unfair? If you have any ideas such as these about the Sacred, even if these ideas are hidden away in your subconscious mind, they will shape the way you approach spirituality, religion, and mysticism.

Or take the hidden assumptions you carry about yourself. Do you think you are a bad person? An unlovable person? Do you think your sins or mistakes overwhelm your good qualities? Do you think you deserve to be punished, or need to be strictly controlled? Do you think you are incapable of becoming a wildly passionate and loving person? Even if people have managed to escape having toxic beliefs about God, it is too easy to hold toxic beliefs about ourselves, especially since we live in such a hyper-cynical, hypercritical society.

Then there are the hidden assumptions people often have about mysticism itself. Do you think it's impractical, or foolish? Do you think it's something only especially holy or saintly people can do? Do you think the idea of seeing or feeling the presence of God is just too good to be true?

These assumptions are just like the assumption of the poor man who believed his wife was on the verge of cheating on him. They may seem real, they may seem overpowering, but they are just assumptions.

An assumption is something that you don't *know* to be true, but *suspect* is true. Since the mystical way is the way of mystery—the mystery of God, the mystery of life's meaning and purpose, and so forth—it takes us to places where certainty is nearly impossible. We cannot be certain about any of the assumptions we have about the nature of the Sacred, or the dynamics of the relationship between human and Divine. We cannot be certain because this is the realm of mystery. But that uncertainty is holy and sacred. It is a place of spiritual freedom, where we can choose what assumptions we believe to be true. We can assume that the universe is an uncaring or unfriendly place, and we can assume that we have no worth in ourselves—and we'll end up like the poor husband, suspicious and angry and prone to headaches. Or we can assume that the universe is radiantly beautiful and filled with love, and we can assume we have the worth and the power to help increase the love and the beauty in the universe. These kinds of assumptions will speed us along the mystical way.

As aspiring mystics, we need to recognize and acknowledge the hidden beliefs and assumptions we carry, especially about God, ourselves, and the spiritual life. We need to take care to replace negative assumptions with positive ones. Why assume God is wrathful or vengeful, when you can just as easily assume God is loving and forgiving? Why assume you are unworthy of Divine love, when you can just as easily assume that you are supremely worthy? Why assume mysticism is impractical, when you can just as easily assume that it is extremely important?

The Mystery Beneath the Assumptions

It's a major watershed experience for a mystic to suddenly realize that the Sacred is not full of abusive anger, but is truly the source of life and light and love. For example, consider the experience of Martin Luther, the Catholic monk who ignited the Protestant Reformation in sixteenth-century Germany. As a monk, Luther was filled with self-doubt and anxiety in his end-less attempts to please a wrathful God. But when he read a pas-sage in the Bible about how God loved and accepted faithful

Uncovering Your Deals

The English singer Kate Bush wrote a song back in the 1980s about making a deal with God. It's something we all do. We all make deals, agreements where we say to God "You do this and I'll do this." Sometimes these deals can be major stumbling blocks to our mystical growth. They may have made sense when we made them, but later on they prove to be problematic.

What are your deals with God? What kind of bargains have you struck with the Infinite? Chances are, your agreements with the Divine are subconscious—they shape your spiritual life, but you are not consciously aware of them. Well, the time has come to drag those agreements out into the light of day. Sometimes toxic agreements, made during childhood, can sabotage the best efforts for spiritual growth.

Here are some possible deals you might be harboring. Do any sound familiar?

"I'll leave you alone, God, and you leave me alone."

"I'll obey my church's teachings, and you won't be angry at me."

"I'll never do anything bad, and you'll keep me safe from harm."

The problem with deals is that they reduce spirituality to a business transaction, and they often rest on an outmoded image of God. These examples reflect the thinking of people who see God as abusive, or as a fairy-tale Santa Claus, rather than as the source of infinite wisdom and love.

Practical Step: *As you meditate, consider what kind of deals you might have made with God, especially when you were young. Write them down in your journal as they come to you. Ask, "Does this way of seeing God reflect my beliefs and values now?" Review your deals with your soul friend or mentor, and consider if you need to update your ways of imaging the Divine to reflect such mystical values as love and freedom.*

people regardless of how good they are, Luther underwent a major experience of mystical insight. He realized that God was pure love, not the agent of anger and rage that his previous religious training had led him to believe. This experience of Divine love proved so powerful that it inspired Luther to set into motion the chain of events that would transform the Christian religion forever.

Take the time to become familiar with your own hidden assumptions about God—and whenever they are in any way limiting or unloving, cultivate a new assumption, a new thought pattern, a new belief, based on the highest principles of love and forgiveness and splendid radiance that you can muster. But don't assume you now have it all figured out. Remember how beneath all our assumptions, whether positive or negative, there remains the uncharted wilderness of Sacred mystery. Whether we like it or not, all our "knowledge" about spirituality is nothing more than a set of assumptions. The spiritual mysteries lie beyond our ability to capture knowledge or certify theories.

We need to be humble about what we know and don't know. Choose to regard the Sacred (and yourself) in as loving a light as possible, and you will be rewarded with an increasing intuitive sense that this is true. Knowing something is intuitively true is not the same thing as having all the answers. So keep a twinkle in your eye. After all, when you affirm that God is love, you are simply saying that the Great Mystery is a great mystery!

In the last chapter we looked at how mystics throughout history have practiced detachment as a spiritual virtue. Often, nonmystics interpret detachment only in terms of material things—to be detached is to reject the desire for wealth or creature comforts. But true detachment goes much deeper than that. To be truly detached is to loosen the hold that assumptions themselves have on our lives. Rather than feeling desperate because of negative assumptions, or Pollyanna-ish because of sunny assumptions, the detached mystic strives to maintain a spirit of openness and childlike innocence when dealing with the mysteries of life. Truly, the nature of the Sacred, or the hidden dynamics of the human soul, or even the potential for mystical union, are all mysteries. The less rigid we are in our assumptions about these mysteries, the farther along we'll be on the mystical way.

The Lure of Magic

We touched on the question of magic earlier, when we considered the "magic" of making a commitment. I said I liked the concept of magic. But magic is a complex and tricky matter, and anyone who walks the path of the mystic will find the promise of magic—the promise of using spiritual power to attain material changes in your life—tremendously alluring. I do believe mysticism makes a difference in life, not just in the theater of the mind, but in real, embodied ways. Therefore, there is an authentically magical element to mysticism. But we need to be careful. Magic, in its allure, can be an addictive dead end just as easily as it can be a force for spiritual liberation.

A generation ago, scientific rationalism was so strong in our society that only a small percentage of people would admit to believing in magic—most people discarded such belief as mere superstition. However, in the postmodern world, quantum physics has turned many of our earlier beliefs squarely on their heads. Brilliant philosophers and scientists from Gary Zukav to Fritjof Capra to Ken Wilber have shown how mystical spirituality complements, rather than contradicts, the frontiers of science, and so belief in possibilities beyond the mechanistic "laws" of normal reality have become closer to the mainstream of human thought. In this quantum world, more and more people are recognizing that magic—the ability to use spiritual power to change the physical world—may not be so farfetched after all.

Magic involves the energy our mind uses, in partnership with the Sacred, to manifest our desires. More traditionally minded religious people focus their magical energy through prayer (and often don't like calling it "magic" at all). Those who follow newer or more alternative paths often explore magic through the use of creative visualization, affirmations, or guided meditations. And people of all paths rely on external objects to help them focus their magical energy—techniques such as lighting a candle, reciting a specific prayer, or burning incense can help a person focus their spiritual energy.

Magic is something that spiritual people either love or hate. In many New Age circles, especially among Pagans and Goddess-worshippers, magic is regarded as an important part of the spiritual journey. Book after book is published on how to develop and refine your magical or psychic powers. But among traditional religions, magic has a much lower reputation. Often, traditional religions either ignore the concept of magic altogether, or else attack it as evil. It strikes me as odd that magic evokes such strong feelings, both pro and con, in people. That makes me think that both sides have only part of the story.

One of the challenges of the mystic way involves learning a balanced view of magic. It's important to understand how creative and wonderful and powerful we really are, and how our ability to believe in and envision a better tomorrow can and does make a difference in our lives. But it's just as important to keep magic in perspective. It is a tool for setting and achieving goals—but it does not automatically make you a better person or a great mystic.

Magic is like a psychedelic drug. On the one hand, it can expand your consciousness and change your perspective on life.

But on the other hand, it can be an addictive dead end. A friend of mine who is an accomplished astrologer tells a cautionary tale: In her younger days, when she was just beginning to study her craft, she became so caught up in consulting the stars that she would cast a horoscope to decide when was the best day to buy her groceries! Thankfully, she came to realize that her reliance on astrology had become a problem, and she worked hard to develop a more balanced perspective. But she is not the only person I've known whose belief in magic has resulted in the person becoming mired in superstitious fear. The fear goes like this: If you don't recite the proper incantation, or light the correctly colored candle, then your magic "won't work"—in other words, your mental and spiritual power is useless. Too many people read tarot cards or consult their astrological charts only to feel highly anxious when they see something that is negative or challenging. It's as if they have surrendered their power and their free will to the stars or the cards. This is magic's dark side, and it is as addictive as any drug.

People with an addiction to magic believe that magical power resides not within their own heart and soul, but outside of themselves—within a particular spell or technique or talisman. This is a sad dead end aspiring mystics need to avoid. Don't waste your time looking for spiritual power in a "cookbook" with recipes for casting spells. Instead, look for your own authentic spiritual power in the only real place where it can be found—in the heart of the Divine Mystery, deep in the love of the Sacred. Magic is not something you do—magic is who you are.

True Magic

I once had a conversation with Kenneth Leech, a prominent English writer on Christian mysticism, about the role of magic in the mystical journey. His comment was that "magic flourishes whenever people lose sight of sacramental spirituality." Of course, as a Christian he had very specific ideas in mind when he used the word "sacramental"—but I believe his comment can apply to people who follow any religious or spiritual path.

A sacrament is an object or ritual that helps us to connect with Sacred love or power. In the Christian tradition, this includes such things as Baptism or Holy Communion. But other traditions have their sacraments as well. In Lakota spirituality, offering the Sacred Pipe to the Great Mystery is a sacramental act. In Judaism, reading the Torah is a sacramental act. In Buddhism, reciting the Diamond Sutra is a sacramental act. In Wicca, drawing down the moon is a sacramental act.

This connects with the real power and purpose of magic— magic not as a catalog of spells or techniques to attain spiritual goodies, but magic as an opening up of our bodies and souls so that spiritual power and love can flow through us, transforming our lives and making a real, positive difference in the world. The difference between sacraments and spells is that sacraments help us to have a deeper *relationship* with the Sacred, while spells function only in terms of *getting something* from the Sacred. A person casts a spell when they want a better job, or a sexy lover, or healing. It's like a business transaction with the gods: "I'll light this green candle and you'll get me money." Well, there's nothing wrong with business, but having a business relationship with a person is not the way to become intimate or to foster love. It's the same way in the spiritual realm. Lighting a candle in order to get something is reducing spirituality to the level of striking a bargain. But lighting a candle to create a warm environment for loving prayer or meditation is another matter entirely. Then it becomes a sacramental candle, and the purpose behind it is not to conduct a transaction, but to foster a loving relationship.

Make an effort to keep a sacramental dimension to your spirituality alive. In other words, look for ways to connect with the Sacred in your everyday life. They can be very ritualistic ways, such as lighting candles, burning incense, ringing a Tibetan bell, or even reading the tarot. Just remember the magic lies not in the object or the ritual, but in the love that flows between you and the Divine. Allow yourself to perform simple rituals with a sacramental dimension—like lighting a candle before you meditate. A simple act like that, over time, can become a powerful window onto heaven. But if "smells and bells" isn't your thing, look for the presence of the Holy in the dance of sunlight, or when you read books of sacred writings or other inspirational literature. Look for the face of God (or the Goddess) in the people you love. Fortunately, almost anything can be a sacrament—almost anything can help us connect with Sacred love or power, if only we cultivate an open heart and a willing mind.

Does this mean we should never mess with magic? Each of us must answer that question according to our own conscience and the teachings of our particular spiritual tradition. As I've already said, I think understanding magic as a way to tap our inner power in partnership with the Sacred is actually quite useful. But if magic is nothing more than trying to cut a deal or strike a bargain with God, think about it carefully. If you met the most beautiful person in the world and had the choice between marrying that person or starting a business with him/her, what choice would you make (I'm assuming you're available when this encounter takes place!)? I don't know about you, but I would clearly choose love over money. I think the choice in the spiritual life between regarding the Sacred as the source of infinite love, or as a resource to be exploited, is much the same choice. If you want to cast spells, do so with this perspective: Don't let your quest for power make you miss out on something far greater—love.

Agreements

Part of being in relationship is the practice of making and keeping agreements. Perhaps this seems obvious. But think of how poorly concepts such as commitment fare in our modern world. If anything, we expect treachery and negligence more than we expect commitment and integrity from people. We view the world through cynical eyes, expecting people to let us down, to double-cross us, to renege. Once upon a time we used to believe that "A man is only as good as his word"—but the gender-specific language used in this saying shows how old-fashioned it is. Nowadays, the common wisdom seems to be, "Get it in writing." We no longer trust a person by her or his word; we no longer expect people to honor commitments or keep agreements.

As sadly true as that may be in the world of business and other mundane activities, a person who chooses the way of the mystic cannot indulge in such a low standard of integrity. God does not get things in writing—but God does expect us to keep our word. If you make a promise to the Great Mystery, plan on keeping it. If you cannot keep the promises you make, then don't expect to get very far in the mystic way.

Here again we see the role that discipline plays in the mature spiritual life. A spiritual practice of any kind will sooner or later challenge a person to make disciplined commitments on a deeper level than the vagaries of emotion. To understand this, consider the most basic spiritual practice of all: marriage. How easy it is to get married—to fall in love, to sparkle with the excitement of romantic and erotic energy, to plan and enjoy a celebration of this beautiful relationship, where the bride and the groom truly get to be stars for a day. But easy as it is to get married, how difficult it is to stay married—especially in a society with a divorce rate of about 50 percent.

Whether a divorce stems from abuse, or infidelity, or mere irreconcilable differences, it represents on a fundamental level the inability of one or both parties to keep their agreement. I don't mean to get moralistic about divorce, and certainly each situation is unique—but in general, it's a useful example of a deeply rooted problem in our society. We don't know how to keep agreements, especially as circumstances change and our emotions get entangled. We don't know how to separate the passions of the present moment from the commitments that were made precisely to help us weather the storms of passion. We need to learn (or relearn) how to make that distinction. We need to give our commitments the honor they are due. Such honor and integrity is necessary in order to make a marriage survive—and is just as necessary in order to keep a spiritual relationship alive and healthy.

In a failed marriage, we always have the option of pinning all or most of the blame on the other person. Playing the victim may work in divorce (and in some cases such blame is justified) but it's not a useful strategy for the mystical life. When we choose to open ourselves up to the Great Mystery, it's nothing at all like the risk of getting hurt by an unfaithful or an abusive lover. If anything, we are taking the risk of holding ourselves up in a bright light where all of our own limitations and imperfections will be totally visible.

The beginning of a person's spiritual journey mirrors the beginning of a marriage. Initially, much excitement surrounds the path of the mystic—there's almost an erotic yearning to lose one's self in the vastness of Infinite love and life. But eventually, the novelty of the ecstatic quest will wear off. As we discover how mysticism is more about ordinary living than extraordinary experiences, we find ourselves facing the unglamorous reality of our own unfinished personalities, angry or afraid or in some other significant way feeling unconnected to the Sacred. What do we do then? How does the mystical life keep making sense, when we realize there's more to being in relationship with the Sacred Mystery than merely having remarkable experiences?

What do we do? We keep our agreements. We honor the basic practices of spirituality—the commitment to pray or meditate daily, the commitment to study, the commitment to participate in a community, the commitment to serve those who are less fortunate than ourselves. These agreements are the building blocks of spirituality; they are easy commitments to take on when we are feeling "high" in the Spirit, but difficult to maintain over the long haul.

Keeping an agreement is more important to the mystical life than *making* an agreement. Again, here is where discipline comes into play. Saying "I want to meditate an hour a day" is not nearly as pleasing to God as the faithful but far less impressive habit of meditating 10 minutes a day, day in and day out. Aspiring mystics are better off when we start small. Don't make a grand commitment that will fall apart at the first sign of difficulty. What good is it to sign up for two hours of meditation a day with every Saturday spent in the soup kitchen—only to have it all unravel a month later? Start with 5 or 10 minutes a day with an hour of service each month. You can always increase your commitments later (when 10 minutes of meditation becomes as automatic as brushing your teeth, it's time to stretch it to 15 or 20 minutes). But better to build yourself up to spiritual fitness than to start out by taking on more than you can handle.

Perspective

So what happens when we just can't keep a commitment? If we've taken on too much, or if circumstances outside of our control make things impossible? This, after all, is the tragedy of many divorces—"I wanted to make it work, but he wouldn't stop drinking"—and even in the spiritual life, we may find that the inevitable changes of life include changes that make our commitments untenable.

Aspiring mystics need to keep agreements and commitments in healthy perspective. We need to remember that all agreements are renegotiable. If I make a commitment with God to spend a half hour a day in silent meditation, but my wife then loses her job and I have to take a part-time job to make ends meet, I may have no choice but to rethink the parameters of my spiritual practice. *And that's okay.* Here's a valuable lesson I learned along these lines, in the early days of my spiritual life. I had a commitment to pray for 20 minutes a day; a commitment which proved somewhat challenging, but not beyond my reach. Then one day, I brought home an eight-week-old kitten. I soon learned that the kitten had no concept of meditation, and saw my motionless figure as a perfect object for pouncing and frolicking. I quickly found myself unbearably distracted by my new pet. What was I to do? Shut up the kitten in the bedroom while I prayed? That didn't work—she just cried and clawed at the door. Despite my best intentions, I felt increasingly frustrated. When I confided this to my soul friend, he just laughed. "Play with your kitten, and pray later!" was his far-too-sensible advice. So I did. Now, over 10 years later, my middle-aged cat is perfectly happy to sleep through my prayer time! The point is simple. Don't allow your commitments and agreements to become so rigid that they become in themselves obstacles to a living relationship with the Holy.

Of course, our agreements should not be renegotiated lightly. With my kitten, I knew that my "prayerful play" was a temporary situation—eventually my cat would mature and I would resume a more centered practice. And I renegotiated my agreement with the help of a spiritual friend—always a good idea, since the perspective of another can prevent us from falling prey to our own blind spots. As is so often the case in the mystical journey, it's a delicate balance between making firm commitments that are not casually broken, and sometimes having to revise our commitments in keeping with changing life circumstances. Keep the channels of prayer and interaction with others open, and you will receive the guidance you need to make, keep, and sometimes rethink commitments.

The Thirst for Silence

Communication is the key to a successful human relationship. In a similar way, silence is the key to a thriving relationship with the Divine Mystery. Not only the silence of meditation (which may be thought of as active silence), but even the silence of not doing anything in particular, which may be seen as receptive silence. Silence is the DNA of the mystical life. To enter into silence means to enter into a world where we may be, without distraction, simply present with all things. The realm of silence invites the mind to slow its frenzied pace, allowing some of the Sacred mystery to peep through the normal clutter of day-to-day thoughts.

Silence has an inner and outer dimension. In other words, silence may come to us both from within our soul and from our external environment. Both dimensions have importance for the aspiring mystic. Both, alas, are difficult to find. Therefore, it is essential to make silence a priority, seeking it in both forms as much as possible every day.

To find outer silence, we need to escape the external world of noisy surroundings. Turn off the television, the stereo, and the computer. Disconnect the telephone and the fax machine. That's right, I said *disconnect*—merely turning off the ringer is no good; you'll still hear the click of your answering machine and you'll be wondering who it could be. Try to find a place in your home away from the constant whirrr of the refrigerator or the heat pump (it's

Unplugging the Noise Machine

We have wrapped ourselves in a blanket of technology. Countless forms of convenience and entertainment fill our daily lives, often propelled by machines, motors, and electronic devices. They all make noise on some level or another. For the city dweller, noise is so omnipresent that to visit a wilderness area, far away from roads or other forms of human technology, means to enter a realm of silence which feels, well, spooky. It's almost as if our dependence on technology requires us also to depend on the reassuring noise our machine-servants create.

For the would-be mystic, escaping the noise of everyday life to enter into a silent place poses a real challenge. Many of the noise-generating items in our life are so essential that there's no turning them off. And while a few heroic souls have moved off the "grid" by living in a rural setting with no electricity, for most of us such a solution simply is not practical.

So how do we unplug the noise machine?

On a daily basis, probably the best solution is the one that monks have adhered to for centuries now: get up in the middle of the night, or extremely early in the morning, to pray. Between 4:00 and 6:00 A.M. the refrigerator might still be whirring, but most of the other noisemakers in our life are blissfully silent.

The other key strategy involves nature. Get out there when you can, even if only once a year. Several full days basking in the deep silence of the wilderness can go a long way toward making the noisy rest of the year much more manageable.

Practical Step: *In your journal, make a list of everything in your life that creates noise. Include home, work, shopping, and entertainment environments; also include the noise you encounter while traveling or commuting. In making this list, also make note of the times in your life, both on a daily and an irregular basis, when silence is most present for you. Knowing where and when to find the silence will make it much easier to reach.*

amazing—once I began to look for silence in my life, I quickly realized how thoroughly our myriad of technological conveniences have undermined the natural external silent state). When all else fails, seek out a place where silence is more carefully preserved, like a monastery or cathedral or library—or, perhaps best of all, the wilderness (if you can manage to get far enough away from other people and traffic). Even the occasional cawing of a bird is more silent than the normal humming and whirring of modern life.

The point behind cultivating a space for external silence in our lives is because it helps us to nurture that all-important internal silence. This is the silence found within the space of a deep breath, a comfortable posture, a mind willing to let thoughts wander off into nothingness. This is the silence of presence.

Think of internal silence as creating a monastery or a church within—a sacred space in your soul where the Great Mystery may be honored and worshipped. The silence within is the altar on which you offer yourself for Divine Union. Because silence is the medium of the spirit, the presence of God within the silence is subtle and easy to miss—the coming of the Holy often feels like nothing more than an almost imperceptible deepening of the silence. But as you become more familiar with the silent spaces of your life, both within and without you, you will begin to perceive such nuances in the emptiness that speak of Divine presence.

Find your silence and sit in it. To explore the riches of receptive silence, remember this is different from meditation. Don't even try to meditate—for that's *doing something*, and it's a great way to undermine the internal silence. Sure, you need your daily meditation practice, that goes without saying. But to really savor the treasures of silence, make room in your daily schedule for silent time without the mental rigor of prayer or meditation.

The relationship between active silence (meditation) and receptive silence is like the relationship between sex and conversation. The most intense intimacy in marriage is the intimacy of sexual union. But if a marriage only consisted of sex, the intensity would prove exhausting! The sex, joyful and ecstatic as it may be, must be balanced by quiet weekend mornings or serene late nights where a gentler intimacy—the intimacy of conversation or of simply being together—can be nurtured. In a similar way, a mystical relationship with the Divine Mysteries needs both the active intention of meditative practice, but also the habit of time spent in relaxed, receptive silence. The mysteries can open up to us as easily in those quiet moments of doing nothing as they can in the intensive alpha-state of meditation.

It may not be easy to find receptive silence in our techno-urban habitat, but it is essential nonetheless. Steal what little moments of silence you can. The quest for silent time is a natural ally to the quest for prayer or meditation time. Remember that not all silent time needs to be kept busy with prayer in order to be spiritually beneficial. Prayer and meditation can each be susceptible to the frenzies of the thinking mind. Prevent that by allowing as much space for receptive silence as possible.

Don't Forget to Dance

The times we spend in silence are usually times for slowing down or being still. Silence is for sitting, or perhaps for slowly walking. That is good. But it is not all. Life is not meant to be only lived in slowness or stillness. Just as life cannot be all sleeping or all eating, so must it not be all contemplating. Therefore, the aspiring mystic needs to balance the cultivation of silence and inner stillness with an ongoing commitment to playfulness and movement in life. Take the time every day to be silent, but don't forget to dance.

Some religious traditions disapprove of dancing, seeing it as a carnal, worldly activity, unfit for children of the light. Without meaning to criticize anyone's path, I think this is a good example of how spirituality can get out of balance. Of course, not all spiritual traditions oppose dancing. Some forms of Christian worship (like the Shakers and some forms of Pentecostalism) even advocate dancing as a way of worshipping God. Other traditions, like the Sufi and Native American spiritual paths, also incorporate dance into their worship lives.

Dancing is a good metaphor for the more active dimensions of life, on several levels. Not only does it remind us, following the example of the Shakers and the Sufis, that a joyous celebration of our bodies makes for a lovely and powerful way of worship—that is to say, honoring the worthiness of the Sacred—but dance also reminds us that the mystical life extends beyond those activities (like prayer or meditation or going to church) that we normally think of as "spiritual." Too often we think of spirituality as a "part" of life, kind of like another hobby along the lines of collecting coins or following our favorite baseball team. We go to church or synagogue or the ashram, we read mystical books, we have our daily practice of silence and prayer or meditation, we take time to help out those less fortunate than ourselves. These are all essential parts of any spiritual practice. But it's too tempting (and too normal in our culture) to think of such activities as the spiritual "part" of life—while being in a marriage, having sex, raising children, balancing the checkbook, being aggressive at work, mowing the lawn, and so forth and so on are the "other parts" of life, subtly implying that these other parts of life are either not spiritual at all or at least less spiritual than the spiritual parts. But this way of splitting life up into compartments is not useful for the mystical journey. Traveling the path of the Sacred seeker is a 24-7 commitment, and requires that we cultivate spiritual awareness at all times of life—when we balance the checkbook as well as when we feed the homeless; when we dance as well as when we sit in silence.

So in arranging your life to make time for silence every day, don't forget to keep dancing and playing and making love and stopping to smell the roses. And just as importantly, don't forget to see these simple, everyday activities as possible doorways into the Divine presence, just as much as your spiritual practices can be doorways as well.

Chapter 8 # The Way of Transformation

So what's the point? Why bother meditating, or praying, or cultivating silence and serenity in our lives? Especially since the possibility of a big, fireworks-quality mystical experience seems so unlikely for most of us mere mortals, why should we bother walking along the mystic way?

The answer does not have to do with powerhouse knock-your-socks-off visions of God, but rather with a more undramatic—yet sure and steady—process of transformation. It makes sense to pursue mystical spirituality because mysticism changes things. An aspiring mystic might have a powerhouse vision—and might not. But in any event, she surely will experience life in relation to the Divine mystery as an ever-opening flower of new transformation.

The mystic way challenges those who want things to stay the way they've always been. It's the way of growth, development, evolution, revolution, and surprises. Mystical spirituality can sharpen your awareness of every new shift and development in your life, from the seemingly insignificant to those that are positively shattering in their impact.

As we progress in the disciplines and practices of spirituality, we do not find our relationship with God settling into some tidy little program that can be easily figured out and understood. What we find is that the mysteries of the spiritual world include many questions that elude the abilities of the rational mind, many "truths" that seem to contradict one another, and many surprises, where things turn out nothing like we expected, but still seem totally in keeping with Divine will. Mystical transformation takes us into the landscape of paradox. This strange and unpredictable country will become our new home, for it is the frontier at the very edge of mystery. Beyond this lies only the unfathomable glories of the mind of God.

Zen Buddhists have an exercise called the *koan*. The Zen master gives the student a koan, which is usually a riddle, a paradox, or a seemingly unanswerable question. For example, one famous koan asks, "What is the sound of one hand clapping?" The student then must take his or her koan back into meditation, exploring the paradox in the hope that it will trigger the mind into enlightenment. The Zen masters recognize that the human organism—and indeed, all of life—is too complex to be mastered by simple effort of reason and intellect. Ultimately, we must not only master that which makes sense, but also enter the frontiers of consciousness where nothing makes sense at all, before we can truly say we have achieved enlightenment.

One of the paradoxes of this stage of the journey is this: There are no guarantees you will ever achieve enlightenment, or mystical bliss, or ecstasy, or the beatific vision (or whatever you want to call it). And yet, the disciplines of meditation, silent prayer, helping others, and living simply are what is required to become enlightened.

Here's another paradox. The Divine represents unity, and therefore changelessness. Yet the mystical journey will never shield you from change. If anything, it will sensitize you, making change all the more evident in our lives.

Fortunately, mystical change is often glorious. The way of the mystic can inspire even the biggest doubting Thomas to trust that all things are pregnant with Divine ecstasy. As we progress in our practice of meditation, prayer, service, and love, we exercise our spiritual muscles, thereby opening ourselves up to notice that Divine ecstasy more and more. Trust me on this one. I am as skeptical as they come, but years of meditation have brought me to the slow recognition that even a world where innocent little girls suffer strokes and other debilitating diseases is a world nevertheless luminous with the love of God. If you find it hard to believe, sit in silence for as much as you can every day. Find a community of people who share your interest in the spiritual path. And make it a regular habit to perform charitable acts for those less fortunate than yourself. Persevere in these basic disciplines, and within six to nine months, you'll begin to see.

Forks in the Road

As we become increasingly open to the life of the mystic, we open up to all the glory and beauty and radiance of this universe we live in, this realm of dancing energy and dynamic patterns of light and sound and color and form. To walk the mystical walk means saying "yes" to the mystery of life. The way of paradox takes us into the unanswerable questions that swirl around love and death and relationship and community. But it transforms those questions. No longer are they terrifying riddles that must be solved; now they become frontier markers that lead to the undiscovered country of Divine presence. The mystic inspires us to allow the ordinary and mundane things of life to suddenly be caught up "into the seventh heaven," which is to say, to be caught up into the radiance of Divine presence and meaning and compassion. And when you begin to notice the shimmering presence of the Sacred in the most down-to-earth parts of your life, suddenly the big mysteries become just another portal through which the love of God may be encountered.

But the life of the mystic entails far more than just the accumulation of spiritual goodies. It is a life that slowly turns toward the Divine light, just as a plant grows toward the sun. And in that turning, you will find your values shifting, your priorities rearranged, your sense of what is good and important slowly transforming in ways that make sense only from the perspective of eternity. You will find, possibly to your great surprise, that a long walk in the park suddenly seems more interesting than going shopping for that new digital camera; or that working in a soup kitchen seems more fulfilling than going to that big sale at the mall; or that a visit to the local nursing home takes precedence over that TV show that up until recently you would never allow yourself to miss. These may seem like simple, almost facile examples—but they serve to point out how the life of meditation and prayer brings forth changes, great and small, that will alter not only the way you see and feel, but will change the very patterns of your behavior.

The shifts you will undergo as an aspiring mystic are, at first, tiny, subtle changes in your outlook and behavior. But over time, these subtle shifts make a big difference. Think about a fork in the road. At first, the two roads that diverge are very close to each other, but as miles go by, the two roads get further and further apart. Ten miles away from the fork, the two roads are, themselves, miles apart from each other. The same rule applies to the choices made in life as we listen more and more to the whispers of the Sacred. A seemingly insignificant choice today might result in major shifts in your life over the years to come. Don't think the little choices you make today are insignificant. Even the tiniest decision can have world-shattering (or world-liberating) consequences.

Mystical spirituality promises abundance and joy and prosperity. In other words, by seeking to conform your life to the life of the Divine, you are opening yourself up for greater joy and abundance to flow within and through you. It's not in violation of your freedom—you still have control over how much joy and passion and wonder and prosperity you will allow to enter your life. If you don't believe you deserve it, or if you don't want it, it won't come! But it *can* come. Spirituality is about possibilities. To open yourself up to the mysteries of the Sacred includes opening yourself up to infinite possibilities—including the possibilities of joy and wonder and beautiful things happening beyond your wildest dreams.

It's so important, I want to say it again: As an aspiring mystic, allow for the possibilities of joy and wonder and beautiful things to happen in your life, beyond your wildest dreams.

Do it! Expect beauty, joy, abundance, and wonder to flow within your life as you shift and expand to live the mystical life. I cannot guarantee how such wonderful changes will occur, and I can probably guarantee that they won't occur in exactly the way you envision them—but I feel confident in saying that such wondrous changes will occur. Pray and meditate, listen for the voice of the Holy and take time to love yourself and others—and then watch out, for amazing things will happen to you and with you.

Visions and Voices

Back in Chapter 2, we talked about the experience of the *numinous*—the moments and experiences of life that usher us to the brink of wonder and mystery. I want to spiral back to that place, for that is truly the heart of mysticism, and the epicenter of spiritual transformation. Sometimes in striving to meditate regularly or to participate in a community or whatever, we can all too easily forget that core essence of the path. Let's take a moment now to remember the centrality of numinous experience: the unexplainable, ineffable encounter with the Divine mystery.

When we have such an encounter with the Great Mystery, we may (although not always) experience direct, powerful extraordinary phenomena, like visions or voices or other forms of intuitive guidance. In other words, not only do we sense the presence of God, but we also receive information, either on an emotional or mental level.

This doesn't happen to everyone. Remember, there is no guarantee you will experience a supernatural vision of God, or hear some sort of psychic voices, or have any other sort of miraculous or extraordinary mystical experience. Not even if you follow all the advice in this book. Remember, too, that one of the first principles for aspiring mystics is to quit worrying about whether or not you ever have a "supernatural" mystical experience. God cannot be controlled, manipulated, engineered, or even predicted. We mortals simply cannot manage or regulate the force that is greater than the entire universe.

But I'm willing to bet that such extraordinary events are *likely*, if not guaranteed. I believe they happen far more routinely than people are used to discussing, and these moments of ecstasy can often come like a tidal wave, overwhelming the ordinary person who seeks to follow the mystic way.

Take my wife's experience as an example. Before we got married, Fran lived with Rhiannon in a house that had been broken into several times. It felt unsafe, but their economic situation prevented them from moving to a more secure neighborhood. Late one night, when Rhiannon was visiting her grandmother, Fran heard a noise in the basement. Fearing an intruder, she went into a panic, feeling isolated and vulnerable. She turned on the lights in the house and checked every room—fortunately, no burglars. She lit a candle and prayed for half an hour, asking for protection and reassurance. Soon she was calm enough to return to bed. In her words, "Finally I fell into a light sleep and in that state between awake and sleep I clearly heard an authoritative voice saying 'Do you think I am going to let *anything* happen to you?' I was immediately filled with such peace and surrounded with such a sense of safety that I was able to sleep. Even when I woke early the next morning I felt as if God himself had spoken to me. I knew I was glowing."

Indeed, when Fran recounted this story to me, several years after the fact, she glowed in the telling of it. Was it just a dream? Just some reassurance her "higher self" manifested? Or a voice from God? In the end, does it really matter? She felt guided, and

Learning to Recognize Guidance

"Be still and know that I am God" wrote King David in the Psalms. Learning to recognize the guidance that comes from eternity often begins with the simple act of learning to sit still and listen. Indeed, this is one culmination of the basic practices of the mystical life: Meditation, prayer, contemplation, and unprogrammed silent time all contribute toward creating an environment where we can simply be still and know.

But once we achieve that stillness, what is it that we seek to know? How can we recognize Divine guidance when it hits us in the face?

There's no simple answer to this question. The word of guidance could come through the voice of imagination, but it could just as easily be couched in the words of a family member. Guidance could appear in the random words in a newspaper ad, or the lyric of a song on the radio. Guidance requires both the raw material of something in our imagination or our environment, and our ability and willingness to interpret the data to discern the leading of the Spirit.

Thus, the best tool for receiving Divine guidance is openness. Be willing to find a doorway to wisdom and insight in any possible corner of your life. Allow anything, even the most mundane of things, to be a possible messenger bearing words from heaven. Into your openness, wisdom from a source beyond you may more freely enter.

Practical Step: *Keep your soul friend informed of any areas in your life where you are seeking Divine wisdom or guidance. Then, share with your friend anything, no matter how small or seemingly insignificant, that seems as if it could contain guidance. Trust the wisdom of your soul friend as a way of confirming or sharpening your own ability to discern. And when something appears to both of you as having the seed of eternal wisdom, be sure to celebrate!*

in that feeling found peace and reassurance, that stayed with her long after that scary night.

If such experiences of extraordinary communication are even somewhat likely, then part of the job of being a mystic is learning how to interpret and make sense of them. Every aspiring mystic needs to know how to respond to such phenomena in a way that is spiritually useful and beneficial.

On the one hand, visions, voices, and guidance need to be taken seriously. When such an experience comes your way, don't just immediately discount it as a psychological trick or hallucination. On the other hand, discernment and careful consideration are equally necessary. Just because we experience some sort of extraordinary sign, does not mean that it comes from God, or that it necessarily contains important information we need to use. We need to remember that a truly holy encounter with the Sacred will not, or should not, result in our ego getting puffed up. Any experience that leads to an increased sense of arrogant self-importance is either not a genuine mystical encounter, or else we have responded poorly to it.

What kind of guidance are we likely to receive? Almost any arena of life could be transformed by the call of the Divine. We may receive guidance about vocation and career, about relationships, about personal behavior, or even about money and material things. One person may feel God is calling him to enter the ministry, while another feels led to change religions. God might call one couple to get married, another couple (whose life is filled with abuse) may be called to split up. Give that money to a charity, or invest it wisely? Again, the leadings of the Spirit cannot be predicted or controlled. Each one of us must learn to discern for ourselves when we feel God is asking something of us.

Discernment

How should we respond to the extraordinary moments of spiritual experience? What's the best course of action when the heavens open up and God becomes visible (or whatever amazing event we may encounter occurs)? Here are a few basic thoughts:

1. Write it down.

Making a record of your spiritual experience helps not only in noticing the moments of ecstasy, but in discerning what the implications of such moments might be in your life. Set aside a special section of your journal, reserved for your thoughts and interpretations as you move along the spiritual path. Anything that feels the least bit God-inspired—be it a dream, a feeling, or a perception—put it to paper. Years from now, you will cherish the words you have written. And don't worry if it seems that words cannot capture the fullness of the experience—for one thing, they can't; and even so, what little you can express in words will usually be enough to help you remember the entire experience.

2. Be patient.

Don't assume that an extraordinary experience means you must take action right away. The Bible asserts that "A day to God is like a thousand years." In other words, you can afford to take time to reflect and discern on the guidance you are receiving, and when you do take action, in the eyes of the Sacred you are still moving quickly and decisively. Taking time is important, for often something that seems obvious at first blush will not stand up to sustained scrutiny—while true Divine guidance really will stand the test of time.

3. Practice discernment with a soul friend.

Make your spiritual choices with the help of a friend or members of your community. On the surface, it may seem almost blasphemous to question the authenticity of a message we receive from the Sacred. "How dare you question me?" we can imagine God asking. But on the other hand, even with the best of intentions we human beings are likely to screw things up—to misinterpret a message we receive from eternity, or worse yet, to confuse our own fantasies for the will of the Great Mystery. If God is truly the source of love and light and life, then God would certainly support us being careful and taking the time to make sure we got it right.

And the way to do that, of course, is by relying on others. This underscores the importance of a soul friend and a spiritual community. Here's a reason for having a tradition to rely on—with generations of seekers having gone before us, we can rely on their collective wisdom to help us discern where we are being led to today. The wisdom of others helps us to confirm our own wisdom, and identify and let go of our own foibles and self-deceptions.

If you feel you have received guidance from the Great Mystery, share the experience with one or two spiritual friends you trust. Take the time to pray or meditate together, according to the customs of your tradition. Allow your friend to ask questions of you and your experience. Notice if the questions make you feel uncomfortable or defensive. Be sure to be as honest as you can in answering your friend's questions and concerns.

Try to reach consensus in coming to understand the meaning of the guidance you have received and the action you should take. If the friend you work with is your minister or spiritual mentor, then he or she may give you specific instructions. Unless they violate your conscience, go with these instructions. Allow yourself to be in a position where you can learn from the spiritual wisdom of others.

None of this is fail-safe. Entire communities have made mistakes in their efforts to follow Divine guidance, and some of the greatest spiritual leaders in history—from Buddha to Jesus to Francis of Assisi and Martin Luther—have made their mark precisely by breaking free of their communities' pre-existing limitations. But as a general rule, the wisdom and discernment of a community—even a community consisting of a single friend—can be a powerful aid in helping to make decisions out of faithfulness and love.

Sacred Challenge

Not all the transformations or calls from eternity that we encounter on the mystic way will be pleasurable and exciting. We are far more likely to be called to lose weight than we are to be called to become a spiritual celebrity who writes best-selling books (trust me, this is something I'm struggling with in my own life!). We love the idea of transformation if it seems sexy and glamorous, but we chafe at the ordinary transformations in which God calls us to grow. And yet, those are the transformations we will certainly and most regularly undergo.

The mystical life will unavoidably challenge us. It will challenge us to evolve, to shed misconceptions and illusions and bad habits, replacing them instead with more mature or evolved or enlightened ways of thinking and seeing and behaving. Whether we like it or not (and I for one tend not to like it when faced with changing something about myself that I would rather not bother to change), the journey on the spiritual path never fails to call forth constructive changes in our lives. These include changes of perception (such as learning to see God in new ways), changes in thoughts and belief (learning to think of the Divine as primarily loving, rather than primarily judgmental), and most challenging of all—changes in behavior.

In the language of traditional Christianity, the spiritual life includes the call to "repent of our sins"—that is to say, to change our lives in such a way that our negative or destructive behavior stops. Other traditions may use less confrontational language, exhorting us to "wake up from our illusions" or to "let go of our negativity," but in the end, all these semantic variations point to the same reality: The Spirit will call each of us to shed those parts of ourselves that don't work, replacing them with more spiritually beneficial qualities and behaviors.

A very brief word about sin: We affluent, educated, sophisticated Americans often have a problem with the concept. We think it is too negative or old-fashioned. Certainly, it is a concept that has been abused by some religious leaders who have insisted that human beings are filled with sin and therefore are evil. But being too preoccupied with our sins is no bigger a problem than a society of people who seem almost universally unwilling to take responsibility for their own actions. We are a society shaped by lawsuits, road rage, and the psychology of blaming Mom and Dad. When something truly horrible happens, such as a shooting in a public school, we work ourselves into a frenzy over trying to determine who is at fault. Have we reached the point where we reject the concept of sin when it applies to ourselves, but remain all too eager to attack the sins of others? Maybe modern society has fallen into this trap, but it is not the way of the mystic. Mysticism requires a certain level of maturity and emotional health, including the willingness to own up to one's own mistakes and errors, and to make amends when necessary.

Every human being is capable of doing things he or she knows (or at least suspects) is wrong or hurtful. The Spirit calls us to shed such unproductive behaviors, to take responsibility for our own actions, and to invest energy in changing ourselves for the better. This is another aspect of letting go—just as we let go of our attachments, so we need to also let go of our hurtful behaviors of any stripe. The old religious language for this is "repentance"—another word that has fallen far out of favor with the sophisticated person of today. Okay, then. Call it "self-improvement" or call it "fulfilling your human potential" or "attaining harmony and balance" or use whatever trendy term feels good for you—but the key is this: *Do it.* Whether we are talking about truly harmful behavior such as a tendency toward violence or abuse; or a minor bad habit such as a tendency toward overeating, the mystic recognizes a common principle: Any behavior that separates us from loving ourselves, loving others, or loving the Sacred, sooner or later needs to be burned away by the mystical fires of the Holy One. So be prepared. Your journey will force you to face the parts of yourself you may not like, you may be ashamed of, you may wish would just go away. Your journey will force you to take responsibility for those parts of yourself, and to commit to the long, slow process of growing beyond them.

Don't Obsess

Important as it is to take responsibility for our own behavior, we also must take care not to obsess over our sins. Preoccupation with sin is as unproductive as the unwillingness to take responsibility for our actions. It seems that for every Johnny who refuses to admit that he has a drinking problem or who has a tendency to "borrow" other people's money, there's a Joanie who is so convinced she is a sinful worm that she lives a joyless and anxious life, driven by her need to measure up to some sort of unattainable goal of holiness and purity.

In many ways, these problems are mirrors of one another—and both are preoccupations with blame: preoccupation with blaming others, or preoccupation with blaming ourselves. Johnny refuses to take responsibility for his own actions, blaming his parents, his boss, or his wife for his poor behavior and his drinking problem. Joanie, on the other hand, has become so enmeshed in a web of self-blame and self-recrimination, that she refuses to give herself permission for any joy or any pleasure in life.

This all stems from not only a poor concept of sin, but a poor concept of God as well. The path of the mystic is not, and never has been, the path of pleasing a raging God—on the contrary, it is the path of loving and being loved by a compassionate God. This is not to say there have never been mystics who have worried about sin or about the wrath of God—but overall, the mystic way is the way of Divine love, not the way of Divine anger. That's an important point to remember, especially if you come out of a religious tradition where Divine anger was (or is) stressed.

We strive to shed our unloving behaviors not in order to *earn* Divine favor, but in *response* to the Sacred love, which is unconditional. We strive to grow and become more compassionate and caring in our lives not in order to make God love us, but because we like ourselves enough to desire the very best—for ourselves. Obsessing on our sins and wrongdoing is an avoidance of responsibility, just like blaming others is. When we obsess on our wrongs, we put all the responsibility on God. God becomes the judge, who decides whether or not we deserve to live. But this is not the role of the Silent Source of Love whom the mystic learns to follow. The God of the mystic is the God who calls us to be mature, to be accountable for our own deeds—and also to accept that mistakes are natural, and even the best of us do things we later regret. Keep it in balance. To use two clichés: Do not let yourself off the hook, but don't sweat the small stuff, either.

Why Angels Fly

Here is a good place to remember the proverbial saying, "Angels fly because they take themselves lightly." We who walk the path of the mystic must always take ourselves lightly, too. And this means taking our sinfulness (or our holiness) lightly.

For that matter, it also means taking our beliefs and our points of view lightly—learning to hold on gently to those words and images and ideas that create for us a sense of security in terms of our relationship to the Great Mystery. This is not cynicism or nihilism—I'm not saying you should believe in nothing, but I am saying that each of us needs to learn to see the openness and fluidity in all of our beliefs, no matter how solid they may seem. Just as a solid object in our physical universe in reality consists of infinite numbers of subatomic particles interacting with great spaces between each one, so too do the dogmas and certainties in which we believe have, in truth, great spaces of possibility and alternative meaning within them all.

Hold your spirituality lightly. Hold your self-image in relationship with God, your behavior, and your experience of the Divine lightly. Most of all, hold your beliefs lightly. Allow for the possibility that the universe, and God, and life, and all things, are far more shimmering and wonderful and radiant and filled with life and love than you may have ever imagined. This is the path of the mystic.

Power, Freedom, and Love

One of the challenges of walking the mystic way is learning to be at peace with the many times in life when God doesn't seem particularly present. Every mystic may have his or her share of numinous experiences, but even the greatest of mystics will live most of their life in an ordinary round of days, without any particularly elevated sense of consciousness or divine awareness. How, then, do we balance the hunger for God's presence with what sometimes feels like God's absence?

The answer lies within. Although we cannot force God to grant us an ongoing sense of Divine presence, we can learn to acknowledge the parts of ourselves that are the most God-like. The Genesis creation myth proclaims that humanity was made in the image of God. Therefore, we can find within ourselves qualities that link us to the Divine. I believe those qualities within every human being that are the most obviously Divine in origin are power, freedom, and love. Even if you never have a gee-whiz experience of God's glory, you can still cultivate a mystical spirituality by acknowledging and honoring these three qualities. To search for evidence of the Divine presence, search for power, freedom, and love—and cultivate these qualities within your own heart as you progress along the way.

The power and freedom of God seem fairly obvious. After all, we are talking about the force that created all things, that "set the stars in motion," to paraphrase Dante, or—to use a more modern metaphor—the force that ignited the Big Bang. In other words, the power of God is a power bigger than the universe itself. Freedom, likewise, must be an attribute of the Sacred, since God is sovereign—in other words, God does not have to answer to anybody. The Great Mystery pulsating through all things simply *is*, without having to depend on anything else for its existence or its destiny.

The love of God may be harder to believe in—especially for people who experience the universe as hostile or uncaring, or who believe that "life's a bitch and then you die." Hopefully, if you have read this far into this book, you are not quite that cynical! A mystic does not avoid the hard and difficult aspects of life, but recognizes that, despite all the pain and suffering, life is essentially a gift from a loving Source. When confronted with pain and suffering, either in ourselves or in others, we can always use it as an excuse to curse God—but a mystic sees it rather as an opportunity to cultivate compassion and healing work. As God has loved us, so we have opportunities to love ourselves and love others.

The Divine is not only larger than the entire universe, but is also knit within every molecule and every cell of our bodies and minds. Therefore, we find God when we find power, freedom, and love within ourselves. This may be the most difficult of all tasks, since the world we live in does not always encourage those kinds of values. Especially in our densely populated and hypercompetitive, business-driven world, we as individuals often do not feel very powerful or free or loving. We seem to get messages bombarded at us every day, encouraging us to feel powerless or constricted or dispassionate. We are encouraged to be passive spectators of media, compliant conformists in the office and at church, and good little consumers of all the many things advertised all around us, worrying more about buying the next essential appliance than about caring for our fellow men and women.

Yet if business, government, and even the church do not empower us, we need to remember that the creative Source of all things is the heart of all power, the origin of all freedom, and the generator of all love. To be in relationship with the Sacred means to connect with the Source of these Holy virtues. And if God is everywhere, it means these qualities reside within our own souls. We are beings of infinite power, absolute freedom, and world-transforming love. We may not realize it yet, or (as I believe is true for most of us) we realize it only partially. But the way of the mystic is the way of cultivating and giving birth to our fullest power (our ability to manifest the things we need and desire), our fullest freedom (our ability to determine for ourselves the course of our life, without needing to comply with or conform to the arbitrary demands of others), and the fullest love (our recognition of deep, soul-level connectedness to others, and our desire to nurture that connectedness in ways that affirm all).

Balancing the Three

We find God when we find power, freedom, and love, whether beyond or within our skin. But we need to find all three of these qualities. Finding just one or two of them is not enough.

Power and freedom without love is the mark not of God, but of a tyrant. Power and love without freedom is the mark of a slave. Freedom and love without power is the mark of a clown. I don't mean to put clowns or slaves down (although I do have a hard time accepting tyrants), but I think it is important to remember that all three of these qualities prove necessary to fully cultivate our own inner Godliness. Part of the mystical journey involves discovering our own capacity to become ever more Divine, as we mature into our spiritual fullness. This means becoming more powerful, more free, and more loving—in equal measures.

A powerful person gets things done. A free person provides leadership and vision. A loving person nurtures others as surely as she nurtures herself. As each of these qualities are knit together, a person begins to manifest more and more of the presence of God, not only for his or her own sake, but for the sake of the entire world. A life filled with power, freedom, and love is a life filled with truth, goodness, and beauty. It is a life shimmering with the radiant presence of the Great Mystery.

The Greatest of These

Love is first among equals. It is so important to the mystical life that it deserves a word or two of its own. The New Testament puts it bluntly, "God is love."

We could ponder the question "What is love?" and quickly fill many books much larger than this one. It's just like the questions "What is God?" or "What is the meaning of life?"—it's a question that vaults us to the frontiers of mystery—the normal habitat of the mystic. C.S. Lewis, the popular Christian apologist, wrote *The Four Loves* late in his life in an attempt to answer this perennial question. As Lewis saw it, love consisted of affection, friendship, eros, and charity. But the kicker is that all four of these loves derive ultimately from the same source, the same portal of mystery out of which all life emerges. Certainly, the spiritual life involves both receiving and giving affection, friendship, passion, and self-sacrifice to the Great Mystery—and out of that transcendent love, finding the fuel for loving other people on Earth.

A mystic is an artist and scientist of love. We long for God's presence like a lover longs for her partner's return. We study and learn so that we may understand the ways of love a bit more clearly. We sit in silence in the hope that the love from on high will whisper in our heart.

Love requires relationship. We relate to the universe, to whatever is beyond the universe that set the stars in motion. We also relate to ourselves, to our planet, to one another in a network of relationship and community. We manage conflict, rejoice in the good times, grieve over the bad times. We celebrate new births and new beginnings, and lament the dying and the lost. Love is

On Falling in Love

In 1986 I heard the controversial priest Matthew Fox speak at American University in Washington, D.C. Among his many provocative stands, Fox advocates a revival of authentic mystical spirituality for Christians (as well as for all people). This particular night, Fox told his audience he thought it was the job of a mystic to fall in love at least three times a day.

What a great image! He didn't just mean falling in love with other people, although that certainly could be part of this process. He meant to fall in love with God, with life, with creation, with nature, with anything and everything that could reveal the glories of the universe to you. By falling in love, you reinvent the glories of mystical spirituality, making the entire universe fresh and new within the vastness of your soul.

So with all due respect to Father Fox, I'd like to pass his advice on. Fall in love at least three times a day. It's nothing you need to force; simply allow the passionate energy to flow through you. Allow yourself to be entranced and enamored of the moments of joy and wonder you encounter. Be vulnerable, willing, juicy, passionate, and erotic in the lightest and purest sense of the word. Then you will fly like the angels.

Practical Step: Use your journal to write love letters. They don't have to be mailed or sent to anyone else; but write them anyway. Write love letters to all the people you love, to God, to yourself, to Mother Nature, to anything and everything you catch yourself loving. Learn to express your capacity to love. Remember, mysticism is about loving. So flex your love muscles!

the core of life. To love is to live—and what the mystic knows, and what we as aspiring mystics strive to know for ourselves, is that all love emanates from the same place, that beating heart at the center of the universe and of all things.

When we meditate, or strive to improve ourselves, or whatever we may do for the sake of our spiritual journey, let us always keep love in mind. Remember that God loves you, whether you feel it or not. Gravity keeps working even when we don't consciously think about it. The love that flows from the center of all things works the same way. It's always there, holding all things together and energizing the flow of the universe. Walk the spiritual path for one reason—to be in relationship with the Source. That is all you need.

The Beatific Vision

We're nearing the end of this little book. In the life of mysticism and spirituality there is no final end, only transition and ever-new beginnings. We are always beginners, and one ending is merely the clearing away of time and space to allow for the next new beginning.

As a way of honoring the cyclical nature of endings and beginnings, let us end where we began—with the *numinous*, the quest for ecstasy and the hope of (to quote William Blake) holding infinity in the palm of our hands and eternity within an hour. As mystics, we are spiritual creatives, endlessly seeking the ultimate alternative—an alternative to the cynical and pessimistic view of life as meaningless suffering, an alternative to the idea that we must be governed by scarcity and competition, an alternative to the idea that God is wrathful and judgmental. A mystic looks both within her soul and beyond the farthest star, to glimpse a rumor of not the way things are, but the way things could be.

According to the classical language of Western mysticism, the goal of a mystic involves the quest for the Beatific Vision—the blessed ability to gaze into the face of God, a vision filled with uncreated light, unlimited beauty, inexhaustible love. To gaze into the shimmering luminous being of the One who exists beyond space and time, beyond the limits of our imagination, beyond the tricks and foibles of language—this, truly, is the goal. All other things that we have discussed over these pages, from study to prayer to discipline to compassion—all derive their strength from the ultimate source, and all ultimately serve to reunite humankind with the bliss of heaven.

To aspire to the mystical life means to believe in the Beatific Vision. For many, perhaps most, of us it may never come in the way we imagine it, but if we keep an open mind and open heart and never stop hoping for it, we will in the end receive the bounty of Divine felicity. If it doesn't come on this side of death, we can trust the reports of those with near-death experiences, those who bring back reports of unspeakable radiance and shimmering joy that await us on the other side. And even if we must wait until the other side of death for the fullness of the Beatific Vision, I believe we are granted glimpses and sidelong glances of glory, here and now.

That may sound like the tired old "pie in the sky" religion that has been used for centuries to keep people in their place. That is not my intent. True, it's a spiritual maxim that even the most glorious or spectacular vision or mystical experience a person might enjoy here on Earth is nothing compared to the joy that is possible beyond the limits of space and time. But we don't have to wait until tomorrow to access Divine joy. Even the tiny glimpses we receive here and now are enough: enough to keep us believing and hoping; enough to inspire us to work hard for a better world, both for ourselves and our children; enough to make life shimmer with meaning, and—dare I say it?—even happiness.

There's a story about two people with a half-filled glass. The optimist sees it as half full, while the pessimist sees it as half empty. Life itself is like a half-filled glass. Each of us has plenty of reasons to believe we've gotten a raw deal. We always have the option to choose bitterness, negativity, or cynicism—to sink into the ever-constricting circle of our own despair. But that's only one way to read the signs. No matter how battered by the circumstances of our life, each of us remains capable of choosing to believe, to hope, and to work for healing and transformation, both for ourselves and for the sake of others. Therein lies the ultimate hope of the mystic: the confident belief that the glass really is half full, but more than that, the hope that life in relation to the Sacred means the glass will, in the end, be filled to overflowing.

Of the Earth

As mystics, how do we make a difference in our world? Few if any of us will become a spiritual celebrity like Sai Baba or some sort of saint or spiritual hero like Mother Teresa. For most of us, the quest of the aspiring mystic is a much more humble matter. Remember, humility means "of the earth." We are called to be earthy mystics as well as aspiring ones.

An old Zen tale talks about the pupil asking the master, "What did you do before you were enlightened?" The master replied, "I chopped wood and carried water." The pupil continued, "And what did you do after your enlightenment?" To which the master replied, "I chopped wood and carried water." Choosing to pursue union with God—to seek after the Beatific Vision, that sense of union in the deep and profound way attained by Julian of Norwich or the Buddha—does not mean we abandon the humble and simple rhythms of life. On the contrary, it means we throw ourselves into them with the gratitude and hope and faith that truly characterizes a person of the spirit.

Wash the dishes. Fold the laundry. Breathe deeply and sit patiently in rush hour traffic. Allow an acquaintance whose mother is dying to interrupt your busy day. Take the time to buy a sandwich for a man on the street, and visit with him while he eats. Chop wood. Carry water. We each have thousands of opportunities to practice the down-to-earth disciplines of the mystical life, thousands of simple and lowly moments where the light of eternity can shine on and transform the most mundane of activities. To be a mystic is to be a detective, always looking for the signs of grace and spirit in every situation, no matter how humble or messed-up it may seem.

Maintain balance and a sense of humor. Angels fly because they take themselves lightly. Humor is lighthearted, and the Sacred dwells in uncreated light. It's not just a pun, it's a description of reality. Hold our beliefs lightly, hold our meditation practice and our attempts to improve ourselves lightly. We need to be light with ourselves, to allow ourselves moments to smile, to laugh, to take a break, even once in a while to cheat on our practice. Meditate on the idea that God has a deep and jolly sense of humor, and loves nothing more than a good belly laugh. It's a healthy corrective to the old notion of the angry, raging old deity. A laughing God is a loving God, and we can enter the Great Mystery through our own capacity to laugh and sing and play. Be silly for the love of the Sacred. It doesn't mean we have to give up our commitments to healing and transformation and our spiritual practice and all those other "serious" aspects of the mystical life. Not at all! Let's simply remember to massage a little bit of levity between all the seriousness. You, and your relationship with the Sacred, and your relationship with others, will all be the better for it.

This is the end. And the beginning. Blessings to you on your journey!

Epilogue

Books take a long time to write. As I write these words, nearly 22 months have passed by since I wrote the first draft of *The Aspiring Mystic*. During the almost two years that this book has been gestating, many wonderful things have happened. My stepdaughter is a teenager now, with a power wheelchair and a boyfriend. Like all teenagers, she clings to me one minute and pushes me away the next. I'm learning to simply allow that process to unfold.

We still get up every morning like monks, to see Rhiannon off to school. Then my wife and I sit in silence. But we recently got a new kitten. Not only does she disrupt our meditation, she disrupts just about everything—including our two older cats.

The more things change, the more they stay the same. But at least we silly human beings learn a thing or two over time. This go-round, my kitten amuses me more than distresses me. I tend to be amused rather than upset when the silence gets disrupted by a terrifying crash from another part of the house. And I give thanks when the kitten decides the best thing to do during meditation is to come and curl up beside Fran or me, quickly dozing off—and purring so loudly that silence goes out the window.

Life is good. When I really stop to pay attention, I notice how everything shimmers with a barely perceptible sense of Divine radiance. For example, this morning before leaving for work, Fran asked me to come look at a spot on the hall wall where the sun was shining in from one of our living room windows. The winter sunlight through the two panes of glass made the wall glow with a richly textured light. Something we see every morning while we're hustling to get Rhiannon onto the school bus or to get ourselves ready for the day ahead. But this morning, we stopped, gazed, and marveled at the beauty of unadorned light. Just for a second it seemed as if heaven itself had invaded our house.

Then Fran left for work, and I turned on my computer to get back to this book.

May your life be filled with similar small miracles. And may you always see the uncreated light that shines within them.

Recommended Books

Here's a baker's dozen of books that can get you started on the road toward a deeper and fuller knowledge of mysticism and experiential spirituality.

Evelyn Underhill's *Mysticism: The Nature and Development of Spiritual Consciousness* (OneWorld Publications, reprint edition 1993), first published in 1911, was the book that first introduced me to the splendor of mystical spirituality. It's a large and intimidating book, written in a formal British style that 90 years later is not always easy reading. But for the person committed to learning about mysticism not just as an academic exercise, but as a matter for personal exploration, this remains *the* essential work.

Morton Kelsey's *Transcend: A Guide to the Perennial Spiritual Quest* (Element Books, 1991) provides a more contemporary doorway into Christian mysticism. Kelsey is an Episcopal priest and a Jungian psychologist, so while this book is clearly

Christian in tone, it is informed by the universal wisdom of depth psychology.

Matthew Fox's *Original Blessing: A Primer in Creation Spirituality* (Bear and Company, 1983) is the book for anyone who thinks Christianity is all about following the rules and has nothing to do with mysticism or soul liberation. Fox, a scholar of medieval theology, uses the ideas of the great German mystic Meister Eckhart to lay out a model for an earth-positive spirituality based on four principles: blessing, letting go, creativity, and transformation.

Karen Armstrong's *Visions of God* (Bantam Books, 1994) is a great way to begin reading the classical mystics themselves. Spiritual writers from ancient times can be hard to read, since their language is often stern and theologically complex. In this book, Armstrong has taken the writings of four medieval mystics from fourteenth-century England—including Julian of Norwich, whom we met in Chapter 2—excerpted key passages, and rendered them into accessible modern translations. Along with Armstrong's perceptive introductions to each of the mystics, this book is a handy and user-friendly way to begin studying the mystical heroes.

Carl McColman's *Spirituality: Where Body and Soul Encounter the Sacred* (North Star Publications, 1997), my first book, provides an overview of several key themes in the spiritual life, such as community, belief, sacrifice, prayer, and change. The book explores the relationship between spirituality and culture, including popular culture. Although written primarily from a Christian perspective, the book explores how the major themes of spirituality are universal in nature.

Paramahansa Yogananda's *Autobiography of a Yogi* (Self-Realization Fellowship, 1981) gives a humble and charming glimpse into the life of a Hindu spiritual master. I first read this book while I was in high school, and it opened up for me the entire sweep of Eastern thought and spirituality. Especially joyful are Yogananda's colorful descriptions of mystical experiences such as *samadhi* ("union").

Entering the Stream: An Introduction to the Budda and His Teachings, edited by Samuel Bercholz and Sherab Chödzin Kohn (Shambhala, 1993) is a superb single-volume overview of the Buddha Dharma, its history, different schools of thought, and major teachings. Although this is not a mystical book as such, it opens the door to the vast world of Buddhism, certainly one of the world's great mystical traditions and vitally important for aspiring mystics of all faiths.

Starhawk's *The Spiral Dance* (Harper and Row, 1979) sets the record straight on the controversial and mysterious world of Witchcraft and Goddess spirituality. Contrary to the common misconception that Witchcraft is devil worship, Starhawk shows how it is actually a manifestation of the world's oldest religion: the worship of the Divine mother, as manifest in the natural world.

Essential reading for anyone who wants their mysticism expressed in a feminine way.

John O'Donohue's *Anam Cara: A Book of Celtic Wisdom* (Cliff Street Books, 1997) brings the ancient mysticism of Ireland into sharp modern focus. A poet and gifted storyteller, O'Donohue gently weaves Pagan and Christian elements of Irish spirituality together to form a tapestry of luminous joy. And yes, Anam Cara is the same word as anamchara—a mere spelling variation separates them.

Thich Nhat Hanh's *Peace Is Every Step* (Bantam, 1991) draws from the deep well of Buddhist wisdom to affirm a beautifully simple approach to mindfulness in ordinary, everyday life. In a series of short meditations, Nhat Hanh's eloquent prose creates the same sense of lightness and spaciousness that he hopes to convey through his advocacy of mindfulness, every step of life's way.

Ram Dass's *Be Here Now* (Lama Foundation, 1971) documents the transition of hippie spirituality from LSD adventures to serious mystical practice. Ram Dass was an associate of Timothy Leary's at Harvard, and an early soldier in the psychedelic era. But like many who followed him, he found acid ultimately limited and traveled to India to plug into the real source.

The result: a gifted, wise, and playful teacher whose delightful book helped an entire generation turn East. The bibliography alone is worth the price of admission.

Avraham Greenbaum's *Under the Table and How to Get Up: Jewish Pathways of Spiritual Growth* (Tsohar Publishing, 1991) makes the beautiful and majestic tradition of Jewish spirituality relevant and accessible to the modern reader. Built around an old Chassidic tale of "The Turkey-Prince," this handbook of the spiritual life provides an amusing, yet earnest, introduction to the universal themes of mysticism in a Jewish context.

Carl W. Ernst's *The Shambhala Guide to Sufism* (Shambhala, 1997) opens the door to the rich tradition of mysticism within Islam. This guide covers both the history and the modern expression of Sufism, including Sufism in the West where it has taken on a more universalistic character.

Naturally, these are but a tiny representation of the many books available on the grand and glorious tradition of mysticism. From works of dense, erudite scholarship down to the simplest manual for personal exploration, the literature of mysticism covers a vast terrain. Your anamchara, your spiritual community, and your local spiritual bookstore can provide further recommendations of books to explore. Happy reading!

Index